K.I.S.S.

Gospel Guidelines For Better Relationships

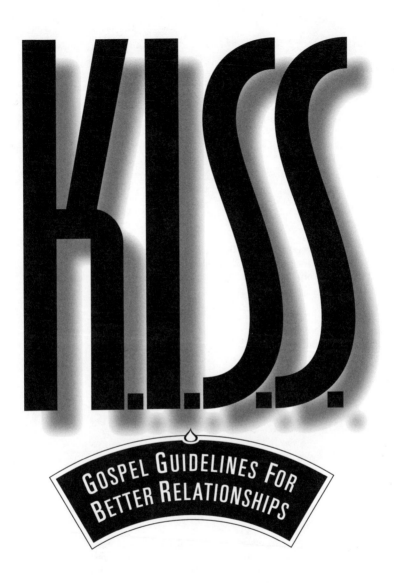

K.I.S.S.

Gospel Guidelines For Better Relationships

Vickey Pahnke

Bookcraft
Salt Lake City, Utah

"The Last Touch." Written by Carol Lynn Pearson.
© Embryo Music (ASCAP), a subsidiary of Excel Entertainment Group, Inc.
From the album "A Time to Love." Used by permission.

Copyright © 1998 by Bookcraft, Inc.

All rights reserved. No part of this book may be reproduced in any form or by any means without permission in writing from the publisher, Bookcraft, Inc., 2405 W. Orton Circle, West Valley City, Utah 84119.

Bookcraft is a registered trademark of Bookcraft, Inc.

Library of Congress Catalog Card Number 98-73149
ISBN 1-57008-539-0

First Printing, 1998

Printed in the United States of America

Contents

1	Introduction.	1
2	K Is for Kindness	8
3	I Is for Involvement	17
4	S Is for Sense of Humor	26
5	S Is for Service.	35
6	Girls Feel, Guys Feel	44
7	I Can't Heeaarr You!.	54
8	Pretty Is as Pretty Does	62
9	Standards: Where Do You Stand?	73
10	Birds of a Feather	83
11	Moonlight and Roses: Romance or Not?.	96
12	Liking Yourself So Others Can Too	104
13	Did You Think to Pray	117
14	It's Worth the Effort	126
	Index.	135

1

Introduction

Why the K.I.S.S. Acronym?

I have taught a class entitled "The K.I.S.S. Principle" for years. It has been a certainty that some new students have thought that we would be examining "Keep It Simple, Stupid" or "Keep It Simple and Sincere" or some other known acronym. Surprise!

To tell you the truth, I can no longer recall *exactly* how this lecture came to be, except that I know lots of people like to kiss and the title would get their attention. Once they were comfortably seated in class, we could cover some territory that is much more important than kissing. Not to undermine the wonderful feelings that kissing is famous for, but we might learn that kissing is not all it's cracked up to be.

Kissing

Before I heard the doctors tell
The dangers of a kiss,
I had considered kissing you
The nearest thing to bliss.
But now I know biology
And sit and sigh and moan—
Six million bacteria,
And I thought we were alone!
—Anonymous

Obviously, a kiss is the topic of many a conversation or the basis for a lot of daydreams. If not the smooching type of kissing, the chocolate-candy type—you know, the ones with the little silver covers, and once you eat one, you have to keep on eating until they're all gone? Then I remembered some words that President Spencer W. Kimball shared once, when he said that kisses are sacred and should not be given out like pretzels (see *The Teachings of Spencer W. Kimball* [Salt Lake City: Bookcraft, 1982], p. 281). *Hmmm, I thought, maybe if I made a correlation between some important values and a subject—or object—on everyone's mind, we could better remember those values. This could be a valuable way of teaching some truths!*

I would not always be around, nor would notes from the class, but people see Hershey's kisses all the time, in so many places. Maybe they could associate that treat with some teachings about real and good relationships! So the K.I.S.S. Principle came to be.

I began taking a bag of those little candies to this presentation so that the students would have a visual image, and I have hoped that whenever they see a Hershey's kiss, their minds go back to a class they might have sat in on a month ago or six years ago.

And so I hope it is with you. As you read the following chapters dealing with each letter of the acronym K.I.S.S., allow the mental picture of that famous candy to form in your mind. Then, long after you have finished this book, you may recall the teachings whenever you see that candy.

It may sound like a silly exercise, but I am of the opinion that if something works to make us better, happier, or more Christlike people, we should go for it. And just for the record, kissing really *is* important, just so long as it is a reflection of what Christ deems appropriate. Consider this scripture found in Moses 7:63: "And the Lord said unto Enoch: Then shalt thou and all thy city meet them there, and we will receive them into our bosom, and they shall see us; and we will fall upon their necks, and they shall fall upon our necks, and we will kiss each other." Note the *Lord* was saying this. To him bestowing a kiss is surely a loving gesture of tender regard and sacred respect, as it should be for all of us.

Now, you and I need to better align ourselves with his teachings, guidelines, and limits. Decide right now, if you have not previously done so, to do as Joshua chose: "As for me and my house, we will serve the Lord" (Joshua 24:15). Making room for him in all our relationships is the key to having better ones. We will have more respect for signs of affection. Our thoughts may be cleaner and our words and actions worthy ones, so that we make more celestial connections!

And you know what? *He* waits to take us in his perfect arms and bestow upon us a kiss of pure and eternal love. After we have learned from mistakes, experience, and study of the scriptures and the words of the prophets, and after we have exercised our earnest desire to improve our relationships. Knowing he awaits us at our journey's end is worth working toward! And while we're achieving better results here and now with our friends, our relationships with Christ will likewise grow better. You cannot lose if you work on the four things this book will discuss.

Before we start working on our relationships, let me tell you a little bit about why I chose to write this book and why I hope you'll be glad you chose to read it.

Why This Book?

This is kind of like a Relationships 099 class. There is no credit for this course, but hopefully we will all learn something helpful. And then, when we start acting on the things we figure out, the world will be full of smiley, happy people. And every day will be like the perfect script for the perfect life. Yeah, right. The truth is, some of your situations won't change at all, but *you will.* I will. It will be easier to get through the bumps and bends and even potholes of relationship problems.

I imagine you as a friend. Actually, you totally *are* my friend—we just may not have met yet. The thoughts for this volume you are reading have been clunking around in my head and heart for a long time. Hopefully some things are written that will benefit you. As in any teaching situation, the teacher learns more than the student. I get to be the teacher here, which is great because I get to learn stuff. So I am saying a prayer and crossing my fingers that you'll find that you will, too, and that you can *relate* better as you go through these chapters.

"The best and most beautiful things in the world cannot be seen or even touched. They must be felt in the heart." You know who said that? Helen Keller, a lady who could not see, could not hear, and was unapproachable for much of her childhood. I love what she said because it is true. For relationships to work, we must learn to better *feel*. A willing heart and a desire to improve are the necessary tools to enjoy the "best and most beautiful things" this world has to offer! In 1 Corinthians 3:13 we learn, "Every man's work shall be made manifest." Our work in relationships will be manifest too. If we work at them, they'll be better ones.

"To exercise is human; not to is divine." Robert Orben made that stellar observation. Some people love physical exercise. The majority are like me—"Uhh, maybe later." How are you at exercising your mind and heart? That one we can't put off without losing out on a better life. By jumping in and learning, working through relationship questions and difficulties, we're saving ourselves problems down the road. Really. And if we learn from others' experiences, from trusted friends and leaders, from scriptural counsel, we save ourselves a lot of hassles. Minna Antrim probably said it best: "Experience is a good teacher, but she sends in terrific bills." True! Learning the hard way is expensive!

I have had some wonderful relationships. There have also been some not-so-great ones. And there have been a few I-don't-ever-want-to-go-there-again ones. Times when I have misspoken, been misunderstood, or miscommunicated my feelings or thoughts have been a bummer. That's when I've felt the heartbreak of missing the mark. On the other hand, I have enjoyed the exhilaration of sometimes connecting heart to heart.

Introduction

I visited with myself at one point and asked, "What has made the difference? What has made some relationships so warm and right that they seemed a dream, while others have been more like nightmares?" The answers did not come all at once. In fact, they are still unfolding and hopefully will for as long as I live. But having pondered—a very important tool in figuring out relationships and everything else—I began reflecting more honestly, leading to *more* questions and *more* reflections. That's good! Because asking questions and going to the right sources allow answers to come.

I have no magic answers for questions like, "How do I make people like me better?" (You *can't;* it's their choice). Nor can I magically answer, "How can I get a date for the prom?" (Ask someone, maybe?), "How can I be more popular?" (Use part of your budget to pay people?), or even "I can't even walk down the hall at school without being swamped by so many girls that I'm late for class—what do I do?" Yes, I *really* have been asked that one before.

I am not a social worker or a counselor. I *am* a person who is probably older than many of you reading this book. And I have the privilege of teaching and speaking with many thousands of you who are perplexed and flabbergasted and amazed as you live and learn about making relationships work. Any teacher in the Church knows that it is not *they* who teach but the *Spirit* who allows us to learn. I'm not writing this book because I've got things all figured out. Far from it. But I do have a testimony of the guiding principles that can make our lives work for good.

I believe you will learn some things that are important for you in your relationships—not necessarily because of what I say, but because as you turn to related scriptures and reflect for yourselves you will gain insight. I have made tons of mistakes and learned a lot of lessons. It has been an honor to gain more insight as I have studied the words of Christ and his prophets. Healing and strength and understanding have come through prayer. I have learned because of so many who have taught great lessons in the best relationships.

Friend to friend, let's walk through some questions and concerns. I'll share with you some real-life examples, some heart-to-heart feelings, and beautiful counsel from the scriptures and our leaders. Please make this a workbook, because relationships take work. I have included space for you to make your own notes and jot your thoughts. Make it your sit-and-think time and your go-and-do space. Then, if you are willing to work on making the concepts fit your lifestyle, you will find your relationships better, more comfortable, and more fun. And more celestial in nature. You'll answer your *own* questions as you receive inspiration.

Get out your scriptures. They are irreplaceable in this adventure we are undertaking. Do you have a pen or pencil handy? And a highlighter? Please keep them nearby. And bring a good attitude for learning as well!

Elder M. Russell Ballard of the Quorum of the Twelve Apostles taught us that "attitude is an important part of the foundation upon which we build a productive life. In appraising our present attitude, we might ask: 'Am I working to become my best self? Do I set worthy and attainable goals? Do I look toward the positive in life? Am I alert to ways that I can render more and better service? Am I doing more than is required of me?' Remember, a good attitude produces good results, a fair attitude fair results, a poor attitude poor results. We each shape our own life, and the shape of it is determined largely by our attitude." ("Providing for Our Needs," *Ensign,* May 1981, p. 86.)

So, why this book? Maybe because I have seen for myself that relationships are absolutely what count most in this life. We all need to feel loved, to feel good about ourselves. All those people we live with and go to school with and stand in line with at the store do too. Because there is always room for improvement, we have an opportunity to grow and improve together as we learn to "hold up [our] light that it may shine unto the world" (3 Nephi 18:24). I am hoping you'll notice a big difference for good in all your relationships, in the family, with your friends, with your sweetheart (or would-be sweetheart), your boss, your*self*, and—most important—with the Savior.

Now, let's venture forth and learn to incorporate the K.I.S.S. Principle (and some other important values) in our lives.

2

K Is for Kindness

Be ye kind one to another.
—*Ephesians 4:32*

K stands for kindness. No rolling of eyes here, please. Kindness is a word that we should probably spend more time pondering so that it is better understood. I'm sure you are kind and thoughtful to your friends and family. Ninety-nine and nine-tenths of the time, anyway. But what if we take a more in-depth look at what kindness is and how it can impact all of your relationships? You have heard the advice to be kind many times in your life. But we are going to further explore being truly *kindhearted,* even when there is nothing in it for you, even when you may not feel like being kind, even when you are feeling bad or sad instead of glad (a brief relapse here in honor of Dr. Seuss!).

I have pretty much decided that there is no such thing as a little thing. Or at least, all those little things can make a *big* difference. If we are the sum total of all the decisions we make and all the little things we choose to say or not say, do or not do, then everything is important, isn't it? If each choice I make today impacts the choices I make next week and next decade, then I am involved in some very important big things. This is not to intimidate you as you live your life on a daily basis but rather to frame for you the thought that *everything counts.*

A few years ago our family moved to Salt Lake City from Virginia. We were excited to move west, but we were leaving family and friends and neighbors we had been close to for a long time. The change was an exciting one for my daughter Andrea. She was just starting high school, and to move across the country was an adventure for her. New location! New friends! New boys to meet! Andrea is a very pretty girl. (I know I'm the mom, but she really is.) So, when she went into Cottonwood High School she was a bit of a threat to some other girls. It made the adjustment a bit harder than it could have been.

In our Salt Lake City ward was a young woman named Mailee. She was a beautiful and loving girl. Her beauty went *all the way through.* (We'll talk more about that later.) Mailee stood apart from the other girls in that she was truly kind to Andrea. She didn't just smile at her, she came up and visited with her. She brought her yearbook so that Andrea could get an idea of the whole school experience. She invited her up to their home. There was always some little thing she did to make Andrea feel more included. She was *kind.* As the years have unfolded, Mailee has proved herself to be a beautiful follower of the Savior, ever kind and thoughtful and gentle. Perhaps Mailee will never know how much my daughter (and I) appreciated her kindness.

President George Albert Smith once counseled, "Every kind act that we perform for one of our Father's children is but a permanent investment made by us that will bear eternal dividends" (in Conference Report, April 1914, p. 13). If we are directing ourselves toward the Savior and conducting ourselves in such a way that the Spirit can attend, we will want to invest in making people happy. We will *want* to do and say things that make others feel good about themselves. And, in turn, we will be happier individuals. What great blessings we would enjoy if we could "so live . . . that each day will find you conscious of having wilfully made no person unhappy" (David O. McKay, "Something Higher than Self," *Brigham Young University Speeches of the Year,* 12 October 1965, p. 8).

What does it mean to be kind? One dictionary's definition is "gentle and considerate in behavior; good-hearted"

(Funk and Wagnalls Standard College Dictionary, 1968). What is your definition? Right here, take out your pen and write a few words that are synonymous with *kind* as far as you are concerned:

_____   _____   _____   _____

_____   _____   _____

Good! Now write the names of three of the most kind people you know:

_____   _____   _____

For what reasons did you choose the names above? How do you feel when you are around those people? Are their characteristics like those President Ezra Taft Benson spoke of when he said: "One who is kind is sympathetic and gentle with others. He is considerate of others' feelings and courteous in his behavior. He has a helpful nature. Kindness pardons others' weaknesses and faults. Kindness is extended to all—to the aged and the young, to animals, to those low of station as well as the high." ("Godly Characteristics of the Master," *Ensign*, November 1986, p. 47.)

Do you see yourself as a kind and loving person? If, at this very minute, someone you know is reading along in this book and penciling in his or her answers, would he or she list your name as one who is truly kind?

As you read and use this chapter on kindness, please understand that I am not advocating doing good, or being kind, in order to make somebody's top-ten list, any more than Moroni ever thought he would serve and obey and endure so that one day his likeness could sit atop the temple. This is about *thinking, pondering, making self-assessments,* and *deciding to do things even better* just because you want to be a kinder person.

In this world it is sometimes cool to be cruel. People learn at an early age to verbally slice others. Taking stabs and cracking sarcastic jokes is expected by many. But not by the Lord. The world says, "Every man for himself." The Lord expects us to come together and help each other like his followers in the meridian of time: "The multitude of them that believed were of one heart and of one soul" (Acts 4:32). The world builds defensive, cold walls around hearts and souls. The gospel of Christ tears down those walls and builds bridges of warmth and love, of kindness. The words of 1 Corinthians 13:4 straightforwardly address our treatment of one another: "Charity suffereth long, and is *kind*" (emphasis added). We know that "charity is the pure love of Christ" (Moroni 7:47). We know that Christ is the great example of loving kindness. Our opportunity, then, is to become more kindhearted. Then we become more like Christ!

What a simple way to create better relationships: be more *kind*. Be more kind than is necessary. Be more kind than you have been before. Be more kind than you think you are capable of being. This allows a sort of growth of spirit as you weigh your words and actions, asking for help in your dealings with others. If you pretty much have this thought in your mind all the time, you are going to be nicer simply because you are thinking that way. Make sense? You will want to be kind just *because*. Not because you want to impress someone. Not because you are forced to be. Not because there is something in it for you (although ultimately there *is*). It feels good to emulate this quality of the Savior. It will make your family and friends happier and your life count for more. And if you are interested in improving your relationships with others, that is certainly a way of making it happen!

If you are a guy, be an absolute gentleman. Opening doors, carrying books, and startling the ladies with your thoughtful gestures might even begin a trend. And once the girls are paying attention to you, your friends will want to enjoy the same attention you are receiving. Does this sound self-serving to you? Guess what. Any time we are being nice, we are doing ourselves a favor. Remember hearing, "What goes around comes around"? It might take a while, but it works just that way. I've heard too many stories of guys who didn't quite fit in when they were younger because they weren't into being so macho. Sometimes the change comes in high school, sometimes not until college, but suddenly Mr. Nice Guy is the one all the girls like. Mr. Tough Guy learns he better smooth some edges if he wants to impress the women.

If you are female, treat the men in your life like true friends. This would include siblings, fathers, grandfathers, friends, would-be-friends, coworkers. Show appreciation for things they do for you. Who doesn't like being appreciated? Enjoy small but significant acts of chivalry. They too are big things when they become part of the whole picture. It doesn't hurt to act decently to everyone, from gas-station attendants to bag boys at the grocery store. Just be nice and friendly. Can you try an experiment? No flirting. No trying to impress. No pouting when you don't get your way. No sneaking peeks in the mirror to make sure everything looks right. For a whole week. Think you can do it? Of course you can. This is how you start being *friends.* You will become known as the girl with the great personality because you are being your *best* self. K stands for kindness, a seemingly small principle with huge rewards!

Several years ago I read an article in the New Era magazine called "The Snob" (Cheryl J. Preece, February 1992, pp. 8–11). It was about a young girl who moved into a new town. She was one of *those* people, the ones with everything going for them. Beautiful and in great shape, she had a good personality and great sense of humor. Her parents were wealthy, allowing her some temporal things that many could not afford. She had it *all.* Therefore, all the other girls (you can fill in the blank here, can't you?) hated her. She had to be a complete snob, they decided. So they set out to make her life miserable. They ignored her, left her out of plans, and made mean remarks. Some of you have moved into a new area and can relate to the feelings the "snob" must have felt. Yet she always smiled, always had a friendly word. That made the girls even more disgusted. Nobody could be this together! The guys thought she was awesome, which upset the other girls even more.

Each month there was a stake dance held. At those dances there was one young man named Foy who pestered all the girls. He was turned down by them every time he asked them to dance, which was often. He was mentally slow and physically awkward, and no one wanted to be embarrassed by being seen dancing with him. Interesting how the traditions of our culture can cause us to do unthinkable things, huh?

The in crowd decided they would set up the "snob" so that she would show her true colors at the next stake dance. *No one* could be as nice, as thoughtful, as *perfect* as she appeared to be. The plan was that when Foy asked the "snob" to dance, which he surely would and probably first, Little Miss Perfect would prove she wasn't too good to be true after all. She would ditch Foy just like everybody else always did.

When the music started that night, our new girl on the block was standing alone on one side of the cultural hall. The in crowd was huddled at the other end. They watched Foy approach the "snob." They watched her smile as she took his arm and moved to the dance floor. Their jaws dropped! Wait a minute, this was a joke. The "snob" would go with him to the center of the floor and leave him there; *nobody* danced with Foy! Then their eyes widened as she continued to talk with him, dancing as though he were the only boy on the face of the planet. And they freaked. No way! Now what were they going to do? If the "snob" danced with Foy, what were they supposed to do when he started in *their* direction?

At the conclusion of their dance, Foy walked his dance partner back to the place she had been standing and started in the group's direction. Who would he pick on first? And what would that person say? Since the "snob" danced with him, they would look *really* bad if they turned him down! Foy approached the first of the group. She looked at her friends in panic, but then realizing she had no choice she allowed herself to be escorted to the floor. Upon her return, Foy went to the next girl, then the next. By the end of the night Foy had danced almost every dance with a different young woman. Amazingly, the girls realized it wasn't so bad dancing with Foy. In fact, it was kind of fun! (Duh. Where do our brains go sometimes?)

An interesting change took place over the next number of months. They began talking to Foy, waving to him in the halls at school and getting to know him as a person. They learned how much there was to love in Foy. At every dance thereafter, Foy never missed a song, always asking as many young women to dance as there were songs played. The girls loved their new friend. Foy passed away a few years later. Among the many friends he left behind were a bunch of girls in the in crowd who were grateful for what they had learned from the "snob." They learned a lesson in *kindness,* a little lesson that means you think of someone else instead of yourself and learn that it all comes back to you anyhow. Just like the girls on the dance floor, you can make a new friend or improve a current relationship at a dance, in your third-period class, on the job, or in your own family. Another interesting thing about the story: we never learned what became of the "snob." The lesson is that it doesn't matter; there is no doubt she was just fine!

My friends, kindness goes a long way. Regardless of our circumstances we can learn a lesson from the "snob." We can choose to be the ones who make a difference in a positive manner. What a simple way to create better relationships! President David O. McKay beautifully taught, "Life is made up not of great sacrifices or duties, but of little things in which smiles and kindness and small obligations given habitually are what win and preserve the heart and secure comfort" (quoted in Conference Report, October 1956, p. 6). He promises *big* blessings for the little daily deeds!

Another example of how easy it can be to show kindness: My son Michael is thirteen. He told me about a girl who attends his junior high who was a little out of sync with most of the others. She listened to music even my young teenager found wild. She was quiet and stayed to herself. He and his friends befriended her and even exerted enough influence to get her to toss out a couple of CDs.

No doubt many of you have done the same type of thing. That story is not out of the ordinary. But Michael's feelings about doing a positive thing were out of the ordinary. He said he felt better inside. He wasn't sure why, he just *did*. "Be ye kind one to another," Paul said in a letter to the Ephesians (4:32).

Wow. Kindness is an action thing. It involves us *doing* something and *becoming* better. Kindness is an all-encompassing word, isn't it? You might want to make a list here, right on this page. List a couple of the attributes you would like to work on starting now. Jot down a couple of things you can *do* to be more kind. For instance, when you're driving, let another car out into the lane in front of you. *That's* kind. Make a phone call and say, "I'm thinking of you!" It'll make their day. Call a company to praise them. That's kind! They're used to complaints. Wash the family car without being asked to. That's kind! On and on we could go. What's going on *your* list?

_____

_____

_____

It is not possible for us to be perfect now, but we can keep trying to be better. As we do something to express kindness, it will make us *feel* better. (See, that word *feel* keeps popping up!) Heaven will be smiling on you as you begin this adventure.

A Few Things You Can Do

- Thank a teacher or coworker (talk about making somebody's day!).
- Mend a broken relationship; call and say something kind.
- *Really* listen when being spoken to.
- State your case gently if you disagree with someone.
- Do something nice without being asked.

- Say thank you, you're welcome, and please, even to your little sister or brother or neighbor who is not at all kind (we'll work on being judgmental later).
- Pray every day to be kind.
- Follow the examples in the scriptures of those who understood this principle.

3

I Is for Involvement

Be ye doers of the word, and not hearers only.
—James 1:22

I is for involvement. OK, this one sounds like it might be easy. Maybe. Let's take a good, close look at what this word means and *can* mean in terms of your life and your relationships becoming better.

Do you not think Heavenly Father sent you into mortality at *this* time and under *these* circumstances to get involved in life, to really be a part of things? There is a popular slogan that says, "He who dies with the most toys wins." We know that isn't so. But there *is* something to be said for more experience gained. Without exception, we become stronger and more confident as we toss aside pride and vanity in order to learn and to enjoy the people and opportunities around us.

Did you ever see that old Church movie called *Cipher in the Snow?* I remember seeing it when I was a fairly new member of the Church. (I joined the Church as a teenager because a *friend decided to get involved.*) It had a profound impact on me. This sweet, little boy got off his school bus one day and just fell over dead. A precious little soul so loved by our Father in Heaven but ignored by so many of his children here. The story touched on the tragedy of being isolated from those around us. If you haven't seen that film yet, please write down in your notes to borrow it from your ward library. Though it was made long ago, its message is probably more pertinent today than when it was made. Why? Because we live in a society largely made up of people who are afraid to get involved, afraid to risk getting out of their comfort zone to help someone else feel more comfortable, afraid to take a deep breath and *jump in* to get more out of life! We are talking about the kinds of things in life that money, prestige, or position cannot buy; the kind of *jumping in* that says "I care," that offers more friendships, more fun, more heartfelt experiences.

Honestly, your desire to get involved may offer some experiences that do not seem to be good ones. (In fact, sometimes being willing to go out on a limb for someone else can be a heartbreaking experience.) But as we will learn, when all is said and done all things have worked together for good (see D&C 100:15) because we loved the Lord enough to truly get involved in this earthly, mortal experience!

Let's place ourselves in a situation we can easily relate to. You are at a stake dance. This is a dance like *many* I have seen. There are a few people out in the middle of the floor. Lo and behold, they are (could it be?) *dancing!* But many are hanging out on the periphery, watching the action in the center of the cultural hall. (We might say they are afraid to get involved.) *I'll ask her to dance the next time a slow song plays,* so many young men are thinking. *Oooohhh, I hope he doesn't ask me to dance; there's no way I'm going out on the dance floor with him!* a few young women may be whining. A bunch of girls are huddled together, giggling or complaining. A number of guys are sitting, some looking utterly bewildered by the whole process, in chairs that are placed like the spokes of a giant, crooked wheel around the dance floor. They are watching the action but are afraid to jump in and become part of it. Oh, there are any number of reasons—or excuses—for not getting involved. But from what I have seen, the people in the middle of the dance floor are the ones having the most fun, making the most friends, and learning the most about self-confidence.

Young women, when a young man asks you to dance, say *yes*. Remember, this is not a marriage proposal, it's a dance! If he persists song after song and you would like the opportunity to dance with lots of fellows (more fun!), then thank him for asking but suggest that maybe a lot of other girls would like the chance to dance and send him off to make another friend. If it turns out to be a horrible three or four minutes (I have to be honest here: for the life of me, I fail to see how one three- or four-minute dance can be *that* horrendous), then chalk it up as your service project for the night. Take a deep breath and silently congratulate yourself for being so benevolent. Chances are great that you will find the guy is, at worst, harmless, and you might just make a new friend. Everyone benefits this way.

OK: Write in below these words, "I will say yes every time a guy asks me to dance at the next stake dance" (this is for the girls, duh) or "I will set a new standard for asking zillions [this might be a slight exaggeration] of girls to dance, and I will have fun doing it!!" (yes, this is for the guys).

_____

_____

The second line is so that you can write the wonderful adjectives that describe the personality of one who would be willing to do such a gallant thing.

Young men: You have to *ask*. Muster up the courage, swallow hard, and go for it. The coolest guys are those who want every girl to feel good about herself, who make it their business to dance with lots of young women in the course of the night, the drop-dead beautiful cheerleader and the quiet little wallflower who seems so out of place. I like that word *wallflower* because a flower is a beautiful creation. Many times it begins as a bud and opens into a beautiful bloom. Many a little bud has bloomed beautifully because of the loving gestures of a few who cared enough to get involved and make her realize how pretty she was. This might sound geeky, but it isn't. I promise: the coolest guys are the ones who make every girl feel like a princess. I have attended youth conferences where I was able to challenge all the young men to ask at least a dozen different young women to dance. It is delightful to watch the action as the floor stays crowded and so many people are involved in the activity.

I once visited with a great group of friends in southern California in which one young man danced with thirty different girls! One at a time, thirty different songs. He said he would have gone for more, but the dance ended. He had a blast. He actively got *into* the activity and had the time of his life. Way to go!

Stay in the middle of things. Contribute to life. Join clubs, offer a helping hand, *talk* to people, be positive. Thank your leaders for their efforts, immerse yourself in the good experiences you are offered. Don't let them pass you by! Be the example. You might be surprised how your actions (or lack of them) may affect so many others.

The story was told of "a fine old New England gentleman . . . [who] used to stop by occasionally at an antique shop in New Hampshire to sell furniture. One day after he left, the antique dealer's wife said she wished she had told him how much she enjoyed his visits. The husband said, 'Next time let's tell him so.' The following summer a young woman came in and introduced herself as the daughter of the old gentleman. Her father, she said, had died. Then the wife told her about the conversation she and her husband had had after the father's last visit. The young woman's eyes filled with tears. 'Oh, how much good that would have done my father!' she cried. 'He was a man who needed to be reassured that he was liked.'

"'Since that day,' the shopkeeper said later, 'whenever I think something particularly nice about a person, I tell them. I might never get another chance.'" (In Paul H. Dunn, *Variable Clouds, Occasional Rain, with a Promise of Sunshine* [Salt Lake City: Bookcraft, 1986], pp. 161–62.)

A great secret to doing better with this principle of involvement may be simply to take the opportunities as they come, getting the most from them and giving the most to them every day, no matter how trivial.

Elder Neal A. Maxwell of the Quorum of the Twelve Apostles has taught us an insightful way of looking at life and all its opportunities: "Baptism by full immersion is best followed by full immersion in the new way of life. Disengagement from the world is best followed by being anxiously engaged in the Lord's work. Hence, there is a counterpart to pausing too long on the edge of the pool of baptism *before entering*—and that is pausing at poolside too long *on the way out*. Reactivated members who have paused on the porch of the Church must not next pause in the foyer. The Holy Ghost can be our constant companion and will confirm our new course, if we so desire. He is prepared to be more than just an occasional friend." (*Wherefore, Ye Must Press Forward* [Salt Lake City: Deseret Book Company, 1977], pp. 3–4; emphasis in original.)

So, this takes us to another whole way of looking at *what ways* we need to get involved. This chapter is not meant to give the go-ahead to any practice or involvement that is not the kind the Holy Ghost could share with you. But you know that. And if you have a few friends who entice you to come along and join in with something (no matter what it may be) that doesn't feel right, that is when you realize that you cannot get involved in *that* because you are involved in *this*, the Lord's kingdom. This is a proclamation you made when you were immersed in the waters of baptism. Your standards of behavior won't allow you to stop in the foyer but lead you to take a front-row seat in the chapel, right up there by the sacrament table (where you *renew* those baptismal covenants every week).

Another word of caution: the world can make things look really good, really inviting. Television and movies take some intriguing points of view. They don't know what we know, my friends. They don't understand how joyful righteous, spiritual living can be. In fact, President Gordon B. Hinckley quoted a newspaper reporter who wrote: "A survey of influential television writers and executives in Hollywood has shown that they are far less religious than the general public. . . . While nearly all of the 104 Hollywood professionals interviewed had a religious background, 45 percent now say they have no religion, and of the other 55 percent only 7 percent say they attend a religious service as much as once a month. 'This group has had a major role in shaping the shows whose themes and stars have become staples in our popular culture.' . . . (*Los Angeles Times,* 19 Feb. 1983, part 2, page 5.)" (Quoted in "Be Not Deceived," *Ensign,* November 1983, pp. 45–46.)

It was 1983 when President Hinckley spoke those words! Imagine what the percentages might be now. And imagine how much faith the Lord has in you, as you are taking your stand *for* good things and *against* shallow, meaningless involvement in things that matter not at all. As we are making our commitment to become more involved in life, we must carefully weigh the things we stand for and the things we cannot.

So, you want to make sure to get more involved in good things and with good people and to do good stuff. Take a few minutes here and list three or four ways in which you plan to become more involved in a great way, OK?

_____

_____

_____

_____

The more you get wholeheartedly involved, the better the quality of life you are going to enjoy. You will know more people, learn more things, better understand yourself and those around you, and have more fun (and be more fun) if you jump on this bandwagon. You will love this bit of advice from Elder Maxwell: "It is so easy to be halfhearted, but this only produces half the growth, half the blessings, and just half a life, really, with more bud than blossom" ("'Willing to Submit,'" *Ensign,* May 1985, p. 71).

I Is for Involvement

Having had the privilege of meeting and teaching so many thousands of young people in so many different areas of the Church, it is clear to me that most of you *are* wholeheartedly desirous of the full blossom of Church activity and spiritual connection with others. As you ponder the ways involvement can improve your relationship with the Savior and with your family and friends, maybe you will receive an inspiration tailor-made for you. You will be more motivated to *do* the things you *know* will be of help in making your desires become reality. The following little triangle is a way I have visualized the importance of turning thoughts into actions (involvement!):

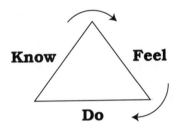

What we *do* is determined by how we *feel* about what we *know*. Think about this. Knowing the truth is not enough to bring us happiness. Knowing in our heads certain principles and practices that will improve our relationships will be of no help if we do not act on that knowledge. Once we internalize something, that principle becomes a value, something that matters enough that we act on it. The principle moves from our heads to our hearts. We *have feelings* concerning the matter. Then we can be "doers of the word, and not hearers only" (James 1:22). Voila, we have become more *involved* in the things we have learned since beginning to gain a testimony of the gospel of Jesus Christ. Pretty neat, huh?

Now, as we finish up this chapter, I hope you feel joyous knowing that the Lord will help you as you take a stab at this involvement thing. Stick to it, and you will see awesome results in your life. I love these words of counsel Elder Marvin J. Ashton offered: "The difference between those committed and those who are not is the difference between the words *want* and *will.* For example, 'I want to pay tithing, but our funds are so limited,' or 'I will pay my tithing.' 'I want to go to sacrament meeting if I have time,' or 'I will go to sacrament meeting.' . . . To reap the full benefits of life, we must fill our days with commitment to worthy goals and principles. There is no other way" ("'The Word Is Commitment,'" *Ensign,* November 1983, p. 63).

There is no other way! We have access to the things that matter most on this earth and in heaven. Is there any reason why you cannot jump in with both feet and become totally involved in the gospel of Jesus Christ? If there is, jot it down. Then examine that reason, study it out, pray about it. You may soon be able to remove it as an obstacle to greater success in this world and with the people in it. The Savior got involved, didn't he? He didn't stand on the periphery, waiting to jump in the middle. He went for it. He did it because he loved; he did it because he was obedient, even when it was not entirely clear to him. As we become more obedient and loving, and thus more involved in good things and with good people, our relationships are going to sprout like we've never imagined! Better, more solid, more fun, more satisfying. Guaranteed. I can make that guarantee because this is another principle based on truth, based on the Lord's own example.

Follow him in this "I" of involvement. And won't you make a better life for yourself? And for so many others who will come to know you and appreciate your good example? Your life will be so much more complete and savory. Imagine the joy you will feel when the Lord can say to you, "Well done, thou good and faithful servant: . . . enter thou into the joy of thy lord" (Matthew 25:21).

Oh, may we each envision that day and go about our involvement in righteous things with that goal in mind!

A Few Things You Can Do

- When you think a compliment, speak the compliment.
- Volunteer to give a prayer in Sunday School class.
- Volunteer to friendship a less-active member.
- Be brave and speak of the gospel to a nonmember friend.
- Create the most awesome family home evening ever.
- Introduce yourself to someone—and smile!
- Make a list of goals you *will* achieve.
- Watch *Cipher in the Snow*.
- Pay attention to someone who seems alone or lonely.
- Pray for guidance in becoming most effectively involved in your family, your ward, your school or workplace, your community.

4

S Is for Sense of Humor

A time to weep, and a time to laugh.
—*Ecclesiastes 3:4*

Toilet paper stuck on the bottom of a shoe.

Being in one of those moods when *everything* is funny.

Getting the joke at the same time your friend does.

A prim- and proper-looking person *almost falls* . . . then looks around to see who might have seen.

The movie you've watched seventeen times and still think is hilarious.

Don't you just love to laugh? And don't you enjoy hanging out with people who have a sense of humor? People who can make you feel better and lighter and happier because they know how to make you laugh? Even hearing someone giggle can make you do the same, can't it? Different people think different things are funny. Our unique senses of humor will cause us to laugh at different situations. But we all love that sound that bubbles up and means we're having fun.

We tend to categorize laughs. All of them are, well, funny. Some people "tee hee" politely, and some bellow with a giant sound that seems to rumble up from the bottom of their toes. Some snicker, and some seem to suck in the very air around them with a scary vacuum-type sound. Others laugh with their entire bodies, while still others clap their hands or hoot and holler. How about the huge fellow who startles you with a tiny, little, high-pitched laugh? No matter the laugh, laughter is music for the soul. What we learn in Proverbs 17:22 is so true: "A merry heart doeth good like a medicine." Laughter is a great help in feeling better about things!

My sister is great medicine for me on many occasions. She knows just what to say to tickle my funny bone and get me going. Sometimes we have a weird chemical reaction that happens between us and we start laughing and laughing and laughing for no real reason at all. And no one else even thinks it's funny, which makes it even funnier to us. Soon the tears are running down our cheeks and we're rocking back and forth in fits of hysteria with red faces and sore smile muscles. It's great!

After this strange virus has run its course and we have regained our composure, we understand that *no one else* would ever get it. It is our personal joke. Long after we have forgotten what set us off, the warm memory of the shared laughter will remain. It's nice to have a lot of those memories. And I appreciate my sister for the gift she has of lifting my spirits and getting a laugh out of me every time.

My daughter and I share this same tendency. It's awesome. Out of nowhere the merriment sneaks in and overtakes us. We get into this odd groove where we breathe at the same time, sniff at the same time, cackle again right on cue as if we had rehearsed for perfect tempo. It is actually kind of scary to anybody watching. But for us problems are temporarily forgotten and we are lost in the hilarity of the moment. We seem to amuse one another. And we tolerate each other's off-kilter sense of humor.

For instance, Andrea has always watched beauty pageants. But not to enjoy the pageantry or watch the talent or even to criticize the contestants. No, Andrea watches the pageant to see if someone is going to trip down the stairs. I'm not kidding. She has this thing about people falling down. If you fall near her and you don't die, she will freak out with laughter. I broke my toe once. It was not a pretty sight. In fact, it was painful and embarrassing. I was vacuuming downstairs. My little toe caught the molding at the corner of the rec room, and there was this odd *snap* noise. I fell over on the floor writhing in pain. (I'm sure I looked intriguing.) Hearing the commotion, Andrea came downstairs. I'll spare you the details, but just suffice it to say that she got a *really good laugh*. And as soon as I regained my composure, I joined in laughing with her.

Because those sorts of things have happened so repeatedly over the years (because I *am* a klutz on occasion and the queen of embarrassing moments!), *I* start laughing when she enters the room, even in my pain! Here's the neat part: The pain goes away, but the memory of the great laugh stays. It has allowed us to be best of friends as well as mother and daughter.

"Laugh and the world laughs with you" is another one of those quotes that has been around forever. Laughing by yourself can be a fun experience. Have you ever gone into the card store and begun browsing through the offbeat, humorous ones? I've found myself laughing out loud before. People look up, connect eye to eye with a go-ahead-and-enjoy—I-do-that-myself type of gaze, and go back to reading (and laughing) themselves! Laughing with other people is even more fun. Maybe it's because we love the sharing of great, fun feelings.

Why is a sense of humor so important in making relationships better? Easy: it makes them more *fun*. Were you up late last weekend? Up with friends? Do you recall laughing with them? Did you notice that the later it got, the funnier things became? And did you awake the next morning and think, *That wasn't even funny?* The more tired we become, the goofier things have a tendency to get. I'll bet you recall plenty of times you have stayed up late with family members and friends and have gotten seriously tickled. Those times, my friends, may be gifts. Gifts of great memories that bind us together and help us lighten gloomy days in the future by recalling heart-lifting thoughts of times past. Days or even months later, you may think back on something and laugh out loud. Life can be tough. Laughter can *tenderize* our hearts and make tough times easier to handle.

It is good for us to have a chuckle. The emphasis is on *good*. Have a good laugh rather than an off-color one or an unnecessary one at another's expense. That isn't humor; that's unkindness, and we've already talked about that. Bad laughs are no laughing matter. If you have been in a place where you have felt uncomfortable because the humor was belittling to another person, remember how your throat seemed to tighten and you felt sad in your heart? How much better it would be for all of us if we could recognize humor for what it is: a way to make us all better and brighter. Really!

A regular person, like you or me, who wants to follow Christ's guidelines will agree with what Elder Neal A. Maxwell said about humor: "A true believer is serious about the living of his life, but he is of good cheer. His humor is the humor of hope, and his mirth is the mirth of modesty, not the hollow laughter or the cutting cleverness of despair. Unlike those of a celebrated devil-may-care lifestyle, his is the quiet heaven-does-care attitude." (*True Believers in Christ* [sound recording] [Provo, Utah: Brigham Young University Sound Services, 1980])

Humor seems to help us balance the small annoyances with a better perspective so that we don't take ourselves so seriously. If I can laugh at myself then I can take a giant step forward in personal and interpersonal development. So, laughter is a *blessing.*

Has there been a time when you have heard off-color jokes and felt forced to laugh in order to feel part of the group? Have you witnessed cutting remarks that hurt another offered under the guise of humor? Some people don't understand the heavenly nature of laughter. Although some have a twisted sense of what is funny, we know better. We know that a sense of humor is a blessing to cherish and a gift worth keeping. When used correctly, it makes life more fun and easier to deal with. Laughter can make relationships more *enjoyable.*

There is an old story of a married couple who had a great sense of humor. One morning the wife awoke her husband, saying, "Honey, wake up! I've had a wonderful dream. I dreamt that you gave me a beautiful ruby necklace! What does this mean?"

He said, "You'll know tonight, my dear!"

The wife was excited when she heard her husband's

car pull into the driveway that evening. She stood at the door full of anticipation. As he entered the house, he handed her a beautifully wrapped package. The wife opened the package to find a book entitled *The Meaning of Dreams*. She laughed uncontrollably, as did he. They shared a great sense of humor, and that gift was more important than all the necklaces in the world. I suspect that sense of humor has seen them safely through some tough situations, making them easier to navigate.

Elder Hugh B. Brown once said, "A wholesome sense of humor will be a safety valve that will enable you to apply the lighter touch to heavy problems and to learn some lessons in problem solving that 'sweat and tears' often fail to dissolve" (in Conference Report, April 1968, p. 100). This gift can turn bad situations around and make good situations even better. It will allow you to take offense less often and alleviate undue stress. It will make you a more likable person.

Some people are born with a quick wit. Some are natural clowns. All of us can develop a nice sense of humor. It can be done by looking for the positive, looking for the humor in a situation. In studying the prophets it is worth noting that they invariably seemed to display a healthy sense of humor and an ability to enjoy a good laugh. Elder Maxwell said it this way: "Humor as a reflection of the incongruities of life can be helpful. The living prophets I have known have all had such a sense of humor." (*Deposition of a Disciple* [Salt Lake City: Deseret Book Company, 1976], p. 52.)

I'm going to share a personal story here. You will feel sorry for me when I finish sharing. This is a true story. You can ask my mom if you don't believe me. I used to laugh exactly like Woody Woodpecker. I'm not kidding. It was scary. When I was really little, my parents would sometimes have to come look at me to see what kind of emotion I was experiencing because they couldn't tell by listening if I was laughing or crying. You can imagine how interesting it must have been for my family.

In second grade I sat beside Paul. I don't remember Paul's last name or what happened on this particular day. I just remember that something happened in class that was really funny. I laughed and laughed. Paul fell out of his seat laughing at *me* laughing, and soon the entire class was in hysteria because I was laughing! I got sent to the principal's office for creating a disturbance in the classroom. Me! Meek and mild *me* who would never want to create any problems or get into trouble. I figured my laugh must be bad and I should not laugh out loud any more. For the longest time I laughed the kind of laugh in which you open your mouth but no sound comes out. It was safer that way. Now, isn't that traumatic? Don't you feel sorry for me?

I know, I know. You're too busy laughing at the mental picture and wondering what my laugh sounds like. I am grateful to announce that I no longer sound like Woody Woodpecker. From all accounts, however, I remain in the bird family; they tell me I sound more like a pigeon these days. Certainly, my laugh is unique. Although I would love one of those feminine, cute ones or a great hearty one, I'm so glad I have this laugh of mine. Laughter is contagious and infectious. What a great virus!

Have you ever been to the movies and sat next to a great big man with a great big laugh? Everybody in the theater was laughing, but not at the movie, they were laughing at the *man* who was laughing at the movie? Isn't it funny how, if one person starts, everybody follows them in laughing? It's great!

There is a wonderful scripture in Genesis: "And Sarah said, God hath made me to laugh, so that all that hear will laugh with me" (21:6). If you read that sentence in context, you will review the story of how Sarah and Abraham finally had a child. They were no spring chickens when that child was born to them. Sarah summed up her amazement and gratitude and wonder at this great blessing by saying God had made her to laugh! Do you not think this laughter was a celebration, a wonderful sound of joy? Oh, that our laughter can be the kind that is a joyful *celebration,* the kind that would never make the Savior uncomfortable were he to join us.

Your sense of humor can allow you to make friends and strengthen those friendships. Who doesn't like to be around someone with a great sense of humor? It is invaluable in creating better relationships when used in a positive way. Common and spiritual sense suggest that we uplift, assist, and turn negative situations around with good humor. You will be better appreciated and better liked if you cultivate that gift.

We hear a great deal about the change of countenance that may come as we take upon us Christ's name and his way of living. He would never hurt another in the name of humor. He would not make a snide remark and then say, "Oh, just kidding!" His way would be to delight in humor being used in a heavenly, helpful way. If you earn a few more laugh lines as you age, good for you! Your countenance is bound to be more inviting and loving if you have sprinkled your character with a good dose of humor. Laughter is good for you and good for those around you. A man named Norman Cousins once said that laughter is inner jogging. A regular exercise program of this inner jogging is bound to make the soul more healthy.

It would make an interesting exercise to go back through your memories of fun times. Write down personal humorous stories. You might be surprised to learn that some of your funniest memories are of things that seemed disastrous at the time. I have heard it said that sometimes *disaster* plus *time* equals *humor.* That holds true for me.

Years ago when my father had just gotten out of the hospital, I was privileged to take him on his first outing, to the barbershop. My home was about a half hour away from my parents', and I was in a rush to get myself ready and drive down to pick up my dad. Have you ever had the feeling that something is not quite right? I was having that uneasy feeling but couldn't figure out why. So I hopped in the car and zipped down to get my dad, and we jaunted off to the barbershop. When we got him situated in the chair, I settled down in a seat to wait. That's when I noticed my shoes. Two different tennis shoes! One was a high-top, and the other was not. Can we say "geek"? I decided to carefully pull up one leg and sit on my foot, thus concealing my preschool attempt at dressing myself that day. No one would ever know. But as I sat there it occurred to me that my father would really enjoy this ridiculous mistake.

"Dad," I said. "Look!" I sat up with both feet on the floor and pointed to my shoes. "Notice anything unusual?"

Dad looked at my feet, at my face, then back at my feet. And then he burst into laughter as he gave me this look that seemed to say, "Bless your heart, some things never change." Everyone in the shop had a good laugh. And I realized that this silly mistake I had made was well worth it since it allowed my father the benefit of a grand dose of medicine! It felt good to share the laugh with him. It was also nice to reinforce the feeling that Dad loved me anyway, regardless of my goofy mistakes.

Similarly, you will find that people love you for who you are, complete with goof ups. As for my outing that day, it has become a great entry in my laughter journal. And it has become a fond and poignant memory, especially since I now must wait till we meet on the other side of the veil to laugh together again. If you are ever feeling down, you can pull out your mental laughter journal and smile as you see the humor in what once was embarrassing.

I once read a Dear Abby column of wedding disasters. People sent in their real stories of unthinkable problems and bizarre occurrences on their big day. I laughed so loudly that my family came running to find out what was going on. (You have to remember I do still have the bird-laugh thing going). The men and women who shared their mishaps had been humiliated, or worse, at the time but now relished the great tale they could share with their children and grandchildren.

And so it is with many things in our lives. Laughter can help us to lighten up, my friends. We can look for humor when it is appropriate and shun it when it is inappropriate. We can accept the gift for what it is.

This S may be more critical to your happiness than you have imagined. The Savior will fine-tune this sense as you sincerely apply it to better your life and the lives of those around you. Good luck! Take a deep breath, close your eyes, and think of something amusing that happened in the last day or two. Remember how nice it was to see everyone smiling and feeling good. Savor it. Make a determination that you will personally be responsible for brightening someone's day by offering the gift of a loving sense of humor. Building on this quality will build your relationships in a great and positive way.

A Few Things You Can Do

- Laugh out loud often!
- Listen for the sound of laughter; appreciate the joyful noise of it.
- Eliminate negative uses of humor.
- Determine never to participate in crude or ugly pseudohumor.
- Tell a silly joke to a child and laugh with him or her.
- Play knock-knock with a little one to help them develop their sense of humor.
- Pray for divine help in developing this sense in a most Christlike way.

5

S Is for Service

*When ye are in the service of your fellow beings
ye are only in the service of your God.*
—Mosiah 2:17

Our final S stands for service. Are we a service-oriented church or what? We speak of service, learn of it, have service projects for Young Men and Young Women activities, and include service as a requirement for Eagle and Young Woman of Excellence awards. With all of this talk about service, is it something we merely give lip service to or do we really understand its significance in building our characters and good eternal relationships?

The world isn't much into service. Oh, we may find a number of kind people along the way, but they didn't learn to be that way from the world. Worldliness seems to bring with it the me-first attitude. Those behaviors are learned early on. "Choose me first!" in kindergarten. "My dad is stronger than your dad!" in grade school. "I've got to be the *best* in the whole group!" in junior high school. "I don't want to be merely *good*-looking; I want to be the *best* looking!" in high school. You might think of different examples, but they all point to "I'm going to watch out for myself first." We eventually move into "Let me cut this guy off and be the first one to stop at the traffic light" as we get older, the old I'm-better-than-you routine. That way of thinking happens without our sometimes even being aware of it. It may be reflected in glances made to friends about others who don't measure up to our expectations or in comments made behind someone's back that only hurt. Sometimes the hurt can be much more than we know.

There was a young woman in my high school that everyone knew not because she was so popular but just the opposite. She did not feel good about herself, and her habits, body language, and lack of friends made it evident. She was tall and big-boned. I like tall, but she didn't and was uncomfortable with her size. Because she took no interest in herself she didn't have those good hygiene habits that make us all more comfortable. Her teeth needed brushing, and her hair needed combing. A month's supply of soap seemed in order. Different tactics were used to inform her of her need to clean up her act (literally). Friends (yeah, right) would leave notes inviting her to take a shower or leave tubes of toothpaste for her to find.

As you are reading this, you can understand that this young woman must have felt really bad about herself. I wish I had realized at the time that those physical manifestations were symptoms of much deeper emotional needs. Then maybe I would have better understood *her* and the need for service.

Her name was Margaret, but somehow a few boys had given her the nickname Monkey partly because she would slump over when she walked. Margaret would sometimes go to extreme measures to gain attention. Her most famous tactic was to pretend to faint in the hallways, always within reaching distance of a few good-looking boys so *they* could be the ones to help her up. It became an odd tradition that from time to time Margaret would do her thing and flail in the middle of the floor. When I look back and realize how far Margaret would go to get a little attention, a touch that would validate her own existence, my heart hurts. In fact, her need for positive reinforcement seems to echo the needs of the little one in *Cipher in the Snow*.

One day I heard a commotion in an adjacent hallway. In my hurry to get to class, I didn't venture over to check it out. But I learned that Monkey Moore was at it again. She had "fainted" right there at the feet of several cute guys. Stopping and bending over her, this cool group of young men decided to help Margaret out. One guy took one hand, a second took the other hand, one fellow took her right leg, and still another grabbed her left leg. They carried her through the hallway like a piece of lumber until they reached the assistant principal's office, where they opened the door, deposited her on the floor, and walked away laughing.

In the last chapter we talked about a good use of humor. How are you feeling about now? Probably like I do each time I think of this scenario: kind of sick inside, right? Well, those guys went on to their next class and never gave Monkey Moore another thought except to spread the word about their little rescue. I heard about what happened. I felt embarrassed about the whole thing. But life goes on, and I finished out the rest of the day without giving too much thought to Margaret's last display or the effect it might have had on her.

The next day no one noticed that Margaret wasn't at school. The following day we learned the rest of the story. That last incident had not gone at all the way Margaret had wanted or needed it to. It was one assault too many for a troubled young lady's tender heart and even more tender emotions. Margaret had been hurt too badly to deal with any more embarrassment or rejection or pain. She had gone home and checked out of mortality.

My mind and heart raced when I heard the news. What if I had taken time to investigate the commotion I had heard in the hall? What if I had put my arm around a fragile girl and told her it was going to be all right, *she* was going to be all right? What if I had looked up her number and given a call to her home to say, "Hi, are you OK?" What if I had done any one of a number of tiny acts of service? What *if*? Maybe it would have made no difference at all. Or maybe it would have made all the difference in the world to one desperately lonely young woman. In my senior year of high school, the same year I joined The Church of Jesus Christ of Latter-day Saints, what if I had understood the concept of service?

We often wait for big ways to show it, but there are hundreds of opportunities around us every day if we look for them and are willing to do it, if we have a portion of

Christlike love that will allow us to think of the other guy and forget about ourselves. "By love serve one another" is what we learn in Galatians 5:13. Small things, simple things done out of love, can make a big difference, for all of us.

Some years ago I was performing a concert for an Especially for Youth session on BYU campus. We had had rehearsal time and were headed for a break before the night's festivities began. A young woman had been watching from the sidelines as we went through our numbers. I saw her watching me now as I headed out. Feeling compelled to stop, I introduced myself. We talked for a few minutes and shared pleasantries. No big deal. I did give her my address and phone number, inviting her to stay in touch with me. After wishing her well, I went on my way.

Several months later I received a letter from that young woman. When I read it, I couldn't believe my eyes. She told me how she had been so depressed that nothing seemed to matter to her anymore. How she was tired of even trying. How she felt so sad and alone that she had entertained thoughts of suicide. I would *never* have known by talking with her! Nor would I have guessed what she shared next. "You were so kind and friendly," she wrote. "You made me feel important. I seemed to be able to feel the Savior's love through you. It made all the difference. Do you realize what an act of service you performed for me?" She detailed some things in her life and how she had made a turnaround. "Now I have great news," she wrote. "I am going to serve a mission! I want to share my love with other people and help them feel the love of the Savior. I want my life to be a life of service." I was shocked! I had done nothing out of the ordinary. *Nothing.* Nothing even worth mentioning. Yet to that one person my tiny act of service had made all the difference. It made me wonder how many times I could make a difference for good if I worked harder at it.

The scriptures say, "Let us not be weary in well doing" (Galatians 6:9). Imagine if I *tried* to be in the service of my fellow beings all the time! What great blessings I would participate in. You too! But what if we get taken for a ride from time to time, offer service to someone who is only taking advantage of us? Here is the best rule of thumb: "It is better to feed nine unworthy persons than to let one worthy person—the tenth, go hungry. Follow this rule and you will be apt to be found on the right side of doing good." (Brigham Young, in *Journal of Discourses* 16:44.)

It is a hard world sometimes. There is a lot of ugliness and mean-spiritedness. There are many among us who are in need of some small act of service that you can provide. Are you willing to make a difference? Even when you're having a bad day? Even when it's hard to do? The poet Robert Browning made a beautiful point when he said, "Ah, but a man's reach should exceed his grasp, or what's a heaven for?" We may not always hit the mark, but we can keep trying to reach beyond ourselves and spread a bit of heaven around! John Wesley once wrote a few lines of thought that say volumes with regard to the importance of service:

> Do all the good you can,
> By all the means you can,
> In all the ways you can,
> In all the places you can,
> At all the times you can,
> To all the people you can,
> As long as ever you can.

At this point you might be thinking, "Hello, Earth to Vickey, I can hardly get through my days as it is. I don't need any more pressure to do even more." We have all felt overwhelmed and insufficient. Whenever those feelings of inadequacy creep in, just remember the Savior *knows* we can succeed. He has faith in us and in our inherent spirituality. As we find time for more service, we will somehow find more *time.* It will work for our good. The adversary's job is to make us feel miserable and unworthy and incompetent. Being of service to someone else lifts our spirits and gives us a can-do attitude, just the kind of attitude people enjoy in another person. Can you see how you are only helping yourself as you help somebody else?

Elder Marvin J. Ashton once said that we "tend to evaluate others on the basis of physical, outward appearance: their 'good looks,' their social status. . . . The Lord, however, has a different standard by which he measures a person. . . . When the Lord measures an individual, He does not take a tape measure around the person's head to determine his mental capacity, nor his chest to determine his manliness, but He measures the heart as an indicator of the person's capacity and potential to bless others." ("The Measure of Our Hearts," *Ensign*, November 1988, p. 15.)

That would include your brothers and sisters, your classmates, the mail carrier, the ticket taker, the cute guy in biology class, or the girl who really bothers you in English. Here is a promise: if you decide to be of service *even more*, you will notice that your circle of friends increases and your quality of relationships improves. Not because the service you render makes others indebted to you, but because you are a better person to be around when your heart is softened by the kneading process of building and lifting others. Great exercise for the heart!

It feels great to lie down at night when we have made a good day. (We don't usually *have* a good day, we *make* it that way!) Serving anonymously makes it even better, because it allows us the opportunity to do something for another person without the desire for recognition or reward. Now, that is service! Do you know that a study was done in Tecumseh, Michigan, that showed that those who regularly do volunteer work have a longer life expectancy? (See *Good Housekeeping*, November 1997, p. 37.) Doing good for other people actually makes us healthier physically and emotionally as well as spiritually. And we know that a loving and concerned Father in Heaven would have it no other way.

That doesn't mean we have to plaster a smile on our face even when we are feeling absolutely lousy. But we

S Is for Service

can measure our words. We can learn to preface a negative comment with a positive one. (I know it's hard, but you will get the hang of it!) *That* can be a service. We can flash a grin at someone who seems lonely. That's a service. We can wave at a passerby. Or take out the garbage without being asked. Or give Mom a big hug. That's service! We can pay attention to others' feelings instead of zeroing in only on our own. As we do so, we will treat our friends better, and potential friends too. The service mode is fun!

When service to your fellow beings (those kids in your P.E. class, your teammates, those students you never talk to, the old people in the ward, and so on) becomes second nature to you, you start to "get it" and enjoy the purposes of this life. You want to help, even if someone has different-colored skin or comes from a different place or sees things in a very contrasting way. At this point you might want to pick up your scriptures again and turn to the story of the good Samaritan found in Luke 10:30–37. Read very carefully about the Samaritan, the supposed inferior to the Jews, who reacted according to his heart. He taught a beautiful lesson in understanding one of the purposes of this life: service. Did you read that a priest and a Levite passed by the wounded traveler? Was it because they were scared? Or too busy? Or did they not think the dying man was worth their attention? We don't know. But we do know that the Samaritan "had compassion on him" (v. 33) and performed a series of services for the virtual stranger.

I love the part that tells us that the Samaritan even left money with the innkeeper to take care of the man he had brought in and promised to repay any additional monies that might be spent on behalf of the injured man. A truly Christlike and selfless person! I bet he had lots of friends. And I bet he worked at valuing those relationships.

I don't know about you, but I hope I get to meet this good Samaritan one day. He teaches us that regardless of *who* we are or *what* our circumstances are, we cannot afford to be too busy, too self-centered, or too apathetic and indifferent to go and do likewise, even to offer a loving hand of service to the Margarets of the world.

God bless you as you exemplify the good Samaritan in your school, workplace, and community. He *will* bless you as he blesses others through you. President Spencer W. Kimball once taught, "God does notice us, and he watches over us. But it is usually through another person that he meets our needs." ("Small Acts of Service," *Ensign,* December 1974, p. 5.) Remember that the next time you feel like you are unappreciated for your efforts or when it seems like you get slam-dunked and misunderstood for trying to offer sincere help to somebody who turns on you. What other choice do we have than to be of service? Without it, we cannot ever know the warm, openhearted feelings that bring us closer to the Lord!

As you practice this principle of service, you will get better and better at it. You will notice an increase in spirituality and happiness, because Christlike service contributes to, among many other things:

1. Righteous personal habits
2. Lack of self-centeredness
3. Increased gratitude quotient
4. Understanding the Savior and his love
5. Our ability to discern
6. Our proximity to the Holy Ghost
7. More loving relationships
8. Others' trust and respect for us
9. Our understanding of Mosiah 2:17

What are some small things you can start doing to show you are seriously interested in taking the Lord's counsel of serving? The Lord said, "He that findeth his life shall lose it: and he that loseth his life for my sake shall find it" (Matthew 10:39). You'll also find a lot more friends and much better relationships as you take to heart the S of service.

A Few Things You Can Do

- Volunteer at a special needs program in the community. Talk about making some celestial friends!
- Write a letter to someone who could really use it.
- Go give a family member a hug right now. Yes, put the book down and go hug!
- Speak to someone you have never met. Just a cheery hello will be great!
- Pray for inspiration as to who really might need your help.
- Listen to the Spirit. He so often directs us in specific ways of service and love.

6

Girls Feel, Guys Feel

*If a house be divided against itself,
that house cannot stand.*
—Mark 3:25

"Why do they *do* that?" It was an exasperated young woman at a youth conference I was attending who asked the question. She was really bugged about the way a young man was acting. She just didn't get it. I'm not sure we solved anything during our conversation, but we had a fun talk. The words she said as we were finishing up stuck with me: "Guys just seem to feel different about a lot of things than girls do." From what I hear and read, men have the same problem with women. How about this for an observation? "Always begin with a woman by telling her that you don't understand women. You will be able to prove it to her satisfaction more certainly than anything else you will ever tell her." (Don Marquis.)

We would agree with the notion that we may not always understand each other. But with gospel tools at our disposal, we can prove more substantial and celestial things as well.

You may have noticed by now that there are differences between girls and guys and that sometimes guys think differently than girls do! That can make for some interesting moments. Fellows, have you ever shaken your head and asked yourself, "Where is she coming from?" Girls, have you ever wondered, "What is he thinking? And how can he be so clueless?" You are not alone in those thoughts.

When I have spoken on this topic I've noticed that

Girls Feel, Guys Feel

lines are drawn and battle stations taken when I ask, "Who has it harder, boys or girls?" There have been some great laughs through the years over statements and sentiments shared. Most girls say it is harder to be a girl. And most guys say it is more difficult to be a guy.

Our job is to come to a better understanding that God's plan includes men and women ("male and female created he them" [Genesis 1:27]) for a divine purpose. We are all better off when we celebrate the differences and share our strengths. That is much more effective than acting as though we are in competition!

Guys will never figure out certain things about girls, such as:

1. Why we have to have six pairs of black shoes in our closet
2. Why we have to go to the bathroom in herds (One girl says, "I think I need to go to the bathroom." Eleven others chime in, "OK! We'll go too!" and they all walk off together.)
3. Why we don't want to be seen in public if our hair is cut one-sixteenth of an inch too much
4. Why we want to talk about *everything*, the more, the better

I could go on and on, but you get the picture. Girls will never get it why young men, when asked, "What's wrong?" almost always say, "Nothing." Or why they would rather eat than do just about anything else. Or why they greet each other with endearing actions such as beating on each other's backs or punching each other in the shoulder. Why do guys bond so well while watching sports? Or playing sports? Or talking about sports? And why do men love to get dirty? And why do they seem to migrate to their own section of a room, no matter what the occasion? Girls don't know.

Girls usually show emotions more. We sometimes cry about everything, or nothing at all. There are certain days when girls just need a good cry. Guys don't understand this. They don't comprehend why we need a really sad movie as our fix so that those tears can fly! (We don't even understand it ourselves; we just enjoy it!) Girls are prone to go up to a friend and exclaim over that new hair cut or new dress—"I just *love* your outfit!" If you can picture a guy doing that, it cannot be a pretty sight! I have seen girls lean forward in a conference or class and start fiddling with the hair of the girl in front of them. No one thinks twice. That is what girls do. But if we saw a guy doing the same thing, it would definitely raise some eyebrows.

Most girls feel that makeup is vitally important. Terms such as *lipstick, eyeliner, mascara,* and *base* are standard in any female restroom. I have known men who know only that *base* is something a player steps on during a baseball game.

Picture this scenario. A young man asks a young woman out. They are at least sixteen, of course. The next day the girl is with her friends. The friends start asking questions about the date. They want to know *everything.* (That is a good thing to keep in mind, guys, when you are dating.) The girl begins, "Oh, it was great! He came over at about three minutes to seven. I wasn't ready yet so he had to wait. I had on the blue outfit, but it didn't look right so I put on my jeans and red shirt. That didn't feel right either, so I finally decided on the yellow matching pants and blouse. The dog jumped on him and got dog hair all over him. My little brother was bugging him and embarrassing me. We went for a hamburger and shake. He smelled so good." And so it goes. Every single detail of the entire night is laid out for the eager friends. The more words shared, the better.

Meanwhile the young man is hanging out with his friends. They ask, "How was the date?" Our guy says, "Fine." Period. End of discussion. Because all those words don't matter. And because somebody says, "Let's go eat," that's what they do!

Rather than fret about the things we don't understand about each other, can't we have a lot more fun and enjoyment if we just appreciate each other? Somehow that has gotten lost in the modern-day, equality-at-all-costs mentality. Undoubtedly the Father created men and women to be equal companions. But it was not intended that the roles of man and woman be interchangeable! Indeed, that would be contrary to his eternal plan.

Here are some observations (and counsel!) we should tune in to:

- "There is nothing in life so admirable as true manhood; there is nothing so sacred as true womanhood" (David O. McKay, *Gospel Ideals* [Salt Lake City: The Improvement Era, 1953], p. 353). *A distinction between manhood and womanhood is clearly made!*
- "No man, young or old, who holds the priesthood of God can honor that priesthood without honoring and respecting womanhood" (N. Eldon Tanner, "Priesthood Responsibilities," *Ensign*, July 1973, p. 95). *The male chauvinistic attitude is not one Heavenly Father teaches!*
- "She who is worthy of the title of lady adorns her mind with the rich things of the kingdom of God; she is modest in her attire and manners; she is prudent, discreet and faithful, and full of all goodness, charity, love, and kindness, with the love of God in her heart" (Brigham Young, in *Journal of Discourses* 17:118). *A real woman supports Christ's ways, not Hollywood's ways!*
- "Brethren, your first and most responsible role in life and in the eternities is to be a righteous husband" (L. Tom Perry, "Father—Your Role, Your Responsibility," *Ensign*, November 1977, p. 63). *The woman's role as wife is equally important!*
- "True men must reach out to show concern for . . . boys," who "need men to look up to, to love and follow. They need men to teach them how to be men or they may learn, as so many do, from imitation men who themselves have it all wrong, who may have perverse ideas, who think that manhood rests in muscles or money, or crime or crudity, or cards or conquests"

(Marion D. Hanks, "Seeing the Five A's," *Ensign*, November 1977, p. 36). *The world's definition undermines the value of true manhood!*

It might be helpful for you to start a list of qualities you think are important in the opposite sex:

_____   _____   _____

_____   _____   _____

Now begin a list of qualities you want to work on in order to be a credit to your own sex:

_____   _____   _____

_____   _____   _____

Please follow the loving advice given in Alma 37:37: "Counsel with the Lord in all thy doings, and he will direct thee for good." As you do so and as you spend more time improving yourself and less time worrying about how much easier the girls or guys have it, you will be amazed at how much more enjoyable and real it is to relate to one another.

I love this anonymous quote: "Enjoy yourself. These are the good old days you're going to miss in the years ahead." This is your time to have fun and gain respectful insight into yourself and more appreciation for the opposite sex. Friendships, romantic flirtations, budding romantic love—we will have many opportunities to exercise our abilities to communicate and relate in a positive way.

When feelings of "I like this person" move into the mode of "I *really* like this person," remember that young men and young women don't always see things the same.

Guys often lock into physical feelings as a way of indicating love. When a girl holds his hand it means she *cares.* Young men, please follow the counsel given in Alma 38:12: "Bridle all your passions, that ye may be filled with love." Physical attraction is powerful and important but not at the expense of creating a much more meaningful (and real) love. You don't want to mistake physical desires for love.

Girls often lock into emotional feelings as a way of indicating love. When a young man talks openly and from the heart, it means he *cares*. Young women, do not overreact when a friend (who happens to be a guy) starts opening up and sharing his inner thoughts with you. It may mean that he is comfortable with you. It may be an indication that he thinks of you as a real buddy. But it may not by any means indicate that he has crossed a line from like to love. We may come from different camps to the middle of the road where love and understanding start.

Girls Camp (Emotional)	Understanding	Boys Camp (Physical)

It takes open communication lines and appreciation for manhood and womanhood to minimize problems. Mixed signals from the young women's camp to the young men's camp can scramble brains and confuse hearts and generally make a mess of relationships! Everyone in favor of having a good time and making good friends and creating good relationships, say aye. The ayes have it! Let's look at some suggestions many of you have shared with me to enjoy the differences between guys and girls:

Guys:
- Act the same when you are by yourself with her as when you are with your friends.
- Listen. I know girls talk a lot sometimes, but listen with your mind as well as ears.

- Be respectful. I promise, any girl worth spending time with will insist that you respect her and her standards.
- Be a gentleman. Girls love you to open doors and such.
- Be creative in your dating. Movies and videos are *borringgg!*
- Have a plan when you take her out; don't make her do all the choosing.
- Inspire her to be a better young woman.

Girls:
- Allow the guys to be gentlemen. And thank them for their efforts.
- Refrain from making comments such as, "I look so ugly tonight!" (What do you want him to say? If he agrees, he is in trouble. If he doesn't, you bring attention to some flaw he probably would never notice.)
- Be on time. It is respectful to be ready when he comes to get you for a date.
- Try not to make a big deal out of everything. Go with the flow.
- Relax. Talk with him as a friend. Learn more about his point of view by asking and listening when he answers.
- Inspire him to be a better young man.

One day you will be ready to step up into a celestial, romantic relationship, having built it upon friendship, mutual admiration, and common desires for eternal goals. It will not hit you like a brick. That is what happens in the movies. Even if the *feelings* do hit you like that, it will take time, effort, prayer, and work to know what love is. One of the most beautiful poems I have read on this subject was written by Carol Lynn Pearson:

The Last Touch

Their first touch . . . was in the park,
and the moon was full.
She was beautiful to him.

And her hair was long and her eyes were blue
and her skin was warm and she turned to him.
And he thought that he knew what love was.

Another touch at twenty two,
on their wedding night
and the stars were bright.
She was beautiful to him.
And her hair smelled sweet and her lips were full
and her skin was warm and she turned to him.
And he thought that he knew what love was.

And then again at twenty five, when the baby came
and the sun was high.
She was beautiful to him.
And her hair was damp and her fingers shook
and her skin was warm and she turned to him.
And he thought that he knew what love was.

Later on at fifty four, sitting on the porch
all the children gone.
She was beautiful to him.
And her hair was gray and her forehead lined
and her skin was warm and she turned to him.
And he thought that he knew what love was.

Their last touch at eighty five was by her bed
and the moon was full.
She was beautiful to him.
And her hair was thin and her eyes were closed
and her skin was cold and she turned to him.
And he knew that he knew what love was.

After sixty eight years of laughter and tears
he Knew that he Knew what love was.

You see, real love is a process that brings us together and lifts us toward God. All the questions and answers and learning that take place when we're teenagers help us better appreciate our role as a male or a female. As men and women learn, laugh, pray, cry, work, and worship together, they move up the pyramid of celestial feelings. Whether you're male or female, these *heavenly feelings* are the same. And they move us in the direction of the third member of any sacred, meaningful love: the Savior, coming closer to him as they love one another in a way acceptable in the eternities.

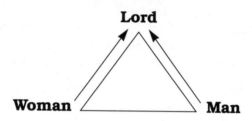

Although girls and guys have a different take on things, there is no need to be frustrated over it. It is the Lord's design that we assist each other in becoming the best we can be. *That* is what matters in relationships. It would be my prayer that each one of you reading this page may work on *yourself*. If you want an "A" man, you need to be an "A" woman, and vice versa. I hope you make wise and good decisions that will lead you to the kind of love spoken of in Carol Lynn Pearson's poem. God bless you as you close the gap between girl and guy feelings and build bridges of understanding, thoughtfulness, and unity. Basing our thoughts and actions on the Savior's example, it will happen!

A Few Things You Can Do

- Get over it; don't *worry* about the differences.
- Concern yourself more with how to make him or her feel better and less with how you look or come across.
- Pray to better understand *your* place as a man or woman.
- Often consult your list of important qualities.
- Relax; you might be making things harder than they are!

- Write down and work toward your goal of celestial marriage; it will make a difference in the way you act and react even now.
- Try *not* to overreact!

7

I Can't Heeaarr You!

Let no corrupt communication proceed out of your mouth.
—Ephesians 4:29

"That is not what I said."
"It is too. I *heard* you say it."
"I did *not* say that!"
"Well, it sure sounded like it."
"Obviously, what you *heard* is not what I *meant*."
"Then speak so I can understand you sometimes. Duh!"

Does any part of that conversation have a familiar ring? If you're like most people, you've either had that conversation or those thoughts, maybe lots of times. Sometimes I have gotten frustrated because I couldn't put into words the things I was thinking. In my mind, it sounded obvious. How come I wasn't making myself understood? And was it me or them?

Did you ever wish you could wave a magic wand and *communicate* clearly? This is what we're talking about in this chapter: communication. How can we have a good relationship with anyone if we don't communicate? That means we do more than say words; we think about them before spitting them out of our mouths, so that they can be understood. And we do more than listen when someone else is talking; we hear what they are saying. In the gospel context, we are concerned about communicating positively and *nicely*.

My mother always said to me, "You catch more flies with honey than with vinegar." That's another one of those sayings with a lot of truth in it. Being sweet (honey) has more pull than being a jerk (vinegar). Even though we are entitled to our feelings, it is important that we not act out against other people *because* of those feelings. Let's examine a few absolutes for sabotaging good communication:

Anger—Anger causes us to lash out and really hurt, even when we don't really mean it. Remember the old adage, "Sticks and stones can break my bones but words can never hurt me"? Well, if we had superhuman tough skins and walls around our hearts, maybe we wouldn't be bothered, but I think most of us relate more closely to this version: "Sticks and stones can break my bones, but words can just about kill me." Anger is an honest emotion, and being human we will feel anger from time to time. But it is the way we deal with those feelings that impacts communication so greatly. You will just love what Elder Neal A. Maxwell had to say about being mad: "Letting off steam always produces more heat than light" ("'Murmur Not,'" *Ensign,* November 1989, p. 84). Enough said!

Emotional overreaction—When we are extremely emotional about an issue, it is more difficult to think clearly because we're too closely tied to it. It clouds everything, including our communication.

The ladies will understand this little communication blurb:

> Male: "What's wrong?"
> Female: "Nothing." (Sniff, sniff.)
> Male: "Something must be wrong; you're *crying!*"
> Female: "No, nothing is wrong!" (Sniff, sniff.)
> Male: "Then why are you crying?"
> Female: "I don't know. I just am." (Sniff, wipe nose, sniff.)

That is a clear-cut case of unclear communication. If it's one of those days when the emotional barometer is off the scale, hey, the best way to communicate is to put your arms around her and tell her you care or keep a healthy distance until things come back around!

Stonewalling—Silence is not always golden. If you've ever known someone who clams up when they get mad, you know how frustrating that silence can be. It is a cold silence, an I-have-built-a-wall-and-you-won't-get-through silence. Think back. Have you reacted this way? Why? Think it through and measure your behavior by one standard: would Jesus do this? We can imagine him thinking things through before he speaks. We can conceive of him measuring his words so they are most clearly understood. But we can't see him shutting himself off from *anyone*. That pretty much settles it; it isn't something for us to do either if we want enjoyable relationships.

Running at the mouth—Have you heard the old saying, "Loose lips sink ships"? Well, they do some pretty good damage to relationships too. If you've ever thought you could *trust* someone and you tell them something no one else should know, only to have them blab the news to half the United States of America, you understand what I'm saying. Being able to share things in confidence with someone, knowing they will keep it to themselves, is a great gift. I have been known to blab on and on nonstop, especially when I'm nervous. Without exception, I have wished I had used the two-two-one theory: You have *two* eyes. You have *two* ears. You have only *one* mouth. Maybe it is better to *see* and *hear* twice as much and *speak* half as much!

If we're jabbering all the time, no one can get a word in edgewise. And we won't learn to be good listeners. Here is some good advice: "Grow antennae, not horns" (James Angell, in *Good Advice* [New York: Wings Books, 1992]). Politely, good-naturedly tune in to the other guy's opinions and thoughts. Save yourself a few battles, and learn more while you're at it.

Dishonesty—If you can't be truthful, you can't build trust. If you can't build trust, you are not going to experience good, positive communication. Anyway, if you really care about someone, you want to speak accurately and honestly. Otherwise, what's the point?

The Dater says, "Uh, I can't go out with you because I, uh, have to go sit with my grandmother who is really sick. Yeah, she's really sick and needs me to stay with her."

The Datee says, "Oh, I'm sorry. You want me to go help out?"

The Dater says, "Oh, no thanks. She might not be comfortable with someone else around."

The Datee decides to drop in at the local burger place. A little while later, the Dater shows up—with someone else. Hmmmm. Might there be a communication problem here? If we care to have Christlike connections to other people, we have to realize that "honesty is of God and dishonesty of the devil; the devil was a liar from the beginning" (Joseph B. Wirthlin, "Without Guile," *Ensign,* May 1988, p. 81). Nephi clearly communicated the beauty of honesty in 2 Nephi 33:6 when he said, "I glory in plainness; I glory in truth; I glory in my Jesus." To have honest communication is to choose as Jesus would. And if you are spending time with folks who don't value honesty, well, you know what to do.

So, you want to improve your communication skills? Do the opposite of what we have been talking about! (Wow, that was deep.) If you suffer from one or more of those weaknesses, pray and work toward doing better. You will! Relationships work better and mean more when we try to communicate in a more Christlike way with everyone we know or meet.

President Spencer W. Kimball once taught it this way: "We must remember that those mortals we meet in parking lots, offices, elevators, and elsewhere are that portion of mankind God has given us to love and to serve. It will do us little good to speak of the general brotherhood of mankind if we cannot regard those who are all around us as our brothers and sisters." ("Jesus: The Perfect Leader," *Ensign,* August 1979, p. 7.)

We have looked at some no-nos. Here are three skills that will help:

First, *take responsibility.* Be willing to say "I'm sorry" or "It was my fault." "I apologize" or "Please forgive me" are excellent also. How about "I made a mistake"? If you do something wrong, admit it. If you forgot something important, say so instead of making excuses. Let's take a look at Luke 15:21: "And the son said unto him, Father, I have sinned against heaven, and in thy sight, and am no more worthy to be called thy son." This parable of the prodigal son teaches, among many things, the importance of owning up to our problems. He goofed big time. He saw the error of his way. He took responsibility and was accepted back and forgiven. Happy endings are good. Taking responsibility will help you turn a corner in your relationships so you can have happy endings too.

The second important issue regarding communication is *respect*. If we properly respect other people even if we don't agree with them or have particularly positive feelings for them, we are going to feel better about ourselves *and* the other guy. Respecting another's position whether they are above or below us on the worldly comparison chart allows us to be more patient and more understanding. The following poem by Ella Wheeler Wilcox teaches some powerful lessons about that:

Lifting and Leaning

There are two kinds of people on earth today,
Just two kinds of people, no more, I say.

Not the good and the bad, for 'tis well understood
The good are half bad and the bad are half good.

Not the happy and sad, for the swift-flying years
Bring each man his laughter and each man his tears.

Not the rich and the poor, for to count a man's wealth
You must first know the state of his conscience
   and health.

Not the humble and proud, for in life's busy span
Who puts on vain airs is not counted a man.

No! the two kinds of people on earth I mean
Are the people who lift and the people who lean.

> Wherever you go you will find the world's masses
> Are ever divided in just these two classes.
>
> And, strangely enough, you will find, too, I ween,
> There is only one lifter to twenty who lean.
>
> In which class are you? Are you easing the load
> Of overtaxed lifters who toil down the road?
>
> Or are you a leaner who lets others bear
> Your portion of worry and labor and care?

If we ever think our position is better than somebody else's, we're headed for trouble. The guy who thinks he's in the power seat can quickly see things change. Respecting people and their rights as individuals will save you on more than one occasion, "more or less"!

The third thought on better communicating: *forgive offenses.* We won't spend a lot of time on that subject in this book (although it's so important we could write novels on it). But I do hope you will think through to the bottom line: if you are harboring bad feelings toward somebody, *you're* the one with the biggest problem. "But do you realize what she *did* to me?" you may ask. Or, "I don't know how I can ever forgive her because it has changed my life forever!"

Somebody may have committed a serious crime against you or a loved one. Maybe an argument has been going for too long. Or maybe you are the victim of an incident in which your name was smeared totally without basis. There are some valid reasons for having negative thoughts about somebody, but keeping the hurt and anger inside only hurts you more. What is done is done. Reliving the hurt or planning to get even only digs a deeper hole, and that is where your energy goes. Trying to get even only makes you just like the ones who did you wrong. Not a good plan. Colossians 3:13 reminds us that we should be "forbearing one another, and forgiving one another, if any man have a quarrel against any: even as Christ forgave you, so also do ye."

Forgiving may not be easy, but it brings you closer to

Christ, and it sure helps you communicate in a more heavenly way. Try remembering what Francis Bacon suggested: "In taking revenge, a man is but even with his enemy; but in passing it over, he is superior."

Communication is pretty tricky. We really cannot have a relationship without it, can we? To do more than speak—to be *understood.* To do more than listen—to *hear.* That takes patience and work. And there is plenty of work to do. If we are willing to do "whatsoever ye do in word or deed . . . all in the name of the Lord Jesus" (Colossians 3:17), there is no doubt that our communication skills will improve and our relationships will too.

As we finish up this chapter, I would like to share with you some words from the poet Daniel W. Hoyt:

> If you have a friend worth loving,
> Love him. Yes, and let him know
> That you love him, ere life's evening
> Tinge his brow with sunset glow.
> Why should good words ne'er be said
> Of a friend till he is dead?

If we have only one shot at mortality, one shot at learning the things necessary for us to get back home with our heavenly parents, don't we need to make our best efforts at *hearing* as Christ would ("If we ask any thing according to his will, he heareth us" [1 John 5:14]) and at *speaking* as Christ would ("As my Father hath taught me, I speak these things" [John 8:28])? Now is the time to love people and let them know it. Right now!

A Few Things You Can Do

- Use the two-two-one theory; note the positive differences in speaking less and learning more.
- Remember Elder Maxwell's words about anger; *think* before you speak so that you accomplish more than just letting off steam!
- Read the entire third chapter of Colossians.

- Sit down with your family all at once or individually and *really* communicate.
- Pray for assistance in communicating in a more Christlike way.
- Time yourself; give the other guy at least thirty seconds of talking without cutting in.
- Practice your skills on your parents and you get a bonus: a better relationship with them.
- Treat everyone with respect—*everyone!*

8

Pretty Is as Pretty Does

The fruit of the Spirit is love.
—Galatians 5:22

Have you ever had a dream in which you were the observer? As a silent overseer, you saw the whole dream-movie from a director's point of view? You were not an active participant in the goings-on, but you saw everything that happened? We need to kind of do that at this point, take a step or two back, breathe deeply, and reflect. It is time for us to get an overview of our lives. That means we become as objective as we possibly can and take a good look at the way we interact with other people.

Are you like me in this way? When someone becomes my friend, they are my friend. I don't think very much about what they look like on the outside because I see them for what they are on the inside. You have probably heard stories of family members who did not notice when another family member made a change in appearance, such as shaving a long-worn mustache or wearing glasses. The truth is, we might notice that something seems different but we cannot put our finger on what it is. That's because we become comfortable on a heart-to-heart basis.

I guess that's a nice thing, really. If all of us were more concerned about how we connected heart to heart, we would be less concerned with our appearances. Because it really is true that pretty is as pretty does. In this chapter we are going to talk about loving—loving everybody—and not being afraid to show it. That means we toss away the notions that someone has to look a certain way (including ourselves) or act a certain way in order to be loved.

Elder Marvin J. Ashton once said that "love should be a vehicle allowed to travel without limitations" ("While They Are Waiting," *Ensign,* May 1988, p. 64). Without limitations. What does that mean? I think you will agree that Heavenly Father has set things up so that there is plenty of love to go around. The arithmetic of love is pretty awesome: you never have to divide it because it can be multiplied over and over again. If we can catch a glimpse of learning to love without limitations, can't we have *huge* numbers of friends? Some we might know well, some we might only pass by. But if there is genuine love in our hearts, it will show in our countenances. And people will see it and be drawn to it, sensing our inner beauty. OK, inner *charm* if you're male and don't want to be referred to as beautiful. Loving without limitations means that we don't decide ahead of time who we will like and who we will not. It invites us to look for the best in everyone. It provides for us to give a guy another chance.

Another chance. Those two words have a good ring to them, don't they? Have you ever at first meeting thought someone was a geek? Have you gotten a first impression that made you think you'd *never* want to hang out with that person again? You might be surprised how much things can change if you don't prejudge.

I met a cute newlywed couple one time when I was on a speaking assignment. When they first met, she thought he ruled. But he thought she was, well, not the kind of person he would want to ask out, not his type at all. But because he was into not prejudging, he *did* ask her out. Then he asked her out again and again. Boy, was he wrong in his initial notion of that girl! They got married, so obviously we see that it was a good plan to give the girl a chance. It's always a good idea to take a little time in deciding who our friends will or will not be! Unless, of course, *they* are way off course. In that instance, there is no need for second thoughts. But you can still love them enough to be nice, act positive, give a smile!

In the overview of your life, what kind of grade would you give yourself on the subject of loving others? Showing by your actions and attitude that you really care about people? If pretty really is as pretty does (and it really is), then what are you doing right? I haven't made fill-in-the-line spaces here, but it would be good to mentally list some things you are doing right. Or jot them in the margins of this page or at the end of the chapter.

What are some things you might change to indicate to others that you understand the worth of those around you? I do a mental checklist every once in a while (probably not as often as I should) to give myself a spiritual face-lift. I figure nothing is better for the face than a genuine smile and a lighter countenance. No makeup can touch it. Money can't buy it. Position cannot enhance it. It is an inner thing, based on acting "pretty" and grounded in the scripture: "A new commandment I give unto you, That ye love one another; as I have loved you, that ye also love one another. By this shall all men know that ye are my disciples, if ye have love one to another." (John 13:34–35.)

If you have ever watched a beauty pageant on television or been a participant in one, it is interesting to wonder if the contestants are only lovely to look at or if their beauty goes all the way through. I heard an anonymous quote once that made me laugh: "Beauty always comes from within—within jars, tubes, and compacts!" I will be the first to admit that I'm grateful for cosmetics. But this French proverb puts things in proper perspective: "Beauty without virtue is a flower without perfume." The makeup on the *outside* cannot make up for less-attractive things such as pride or shallowness on the *inside*. In our family we always hope the girl who wins the crown will be one who is pretty all the way through!

I want you to know of my certainty that beauty is in the eye of the beholder. And when people are kind, loving, and caring they *do* take on a beauty that far surpasses the looks of any gorgeous girl or guy.

An incident that happened a number of years back helped me realize full well how foolish it is to judge based on outward appearance instead of the stuff a person is really made of. In 1991 my sister and I were in the hall outside the intensive care unit at the hospital where my father was a patient. Mom was in with him. Teresa and I were tired, bored, worried, and a little punchy. We saw a lady coming down the hall who looked—I am not kidding—like a bag lady of the first degree. Her hair was a mess, she had on no makeup, her eyes were ringed with dark circles, and she looked like she was caught up in her own world. We looked at each other and grinned. When the lady went past us, we remarked on how she could be a decent-looking woman if only she would take a little more care, if only she would work at it.

Shortly she came back down the hall and then entered the intensive care unit. We wondered how she was able to just walk right in unannounced. We were soon to be put in our place. My mom came out with the bag lady, and she was my dad's heart specialist. She came and put her arms around us and spoke in heartfelt words about her concern for my father. She was a person of charity and great works. Her hair was disheveled because she was more concerned about her patients than her mere outward appearance. Her poor little eyes were dark for want of sleep. She was a person of character and integrity. Oh, how she changed in appearance before my very eyes! How beautiful she was! And how ashamed I felt for being so petty and foolish. That noble lady was indeed pretty all the way through.

The Savior said, "Judge not, that ye be not judged" (Matthew 7:1). Brothers and sisters, I promise you that you don't want to be on the wrong side of the line on this one. If pretty is as pretty does, please do not make snap judgments about other people. So many times we miss the mark if we fail to look with love. There is so much to love in others, even so many of the creepy, grouchy ones. We look better to them and they to us when we look for the beauty within. If this is a big beauty pageant, then let's all be finalists! (What a picture I have in my mind as I consider this contest and envision a whole continent full of finalists, those who understand how true beauty works!) As a decisive pointer for refraining from judging, I love the words of Elder ElRay L. Christiansen, Assistant to the Council of the Twelve Apostles: "The more perfect one becomes, the less he is inclined to speak of the imperfections of others" (in Conference Report, April 1956, p. 114).

Here are a few thoughts for your personal inner-beauty regimen:

Attitude Counts

Attitude really does count. It is sometimes called temperament or disposition. Better yet, we can think of it as the spirit we carry with us. What does your attitude say about you? Do you allow petty things to bring you down and sour your mood? Or are you good about jumping in with a positive outlook? If you find yourself whining or grouching, turn it around. Get an attitude adjustment when you need one. Tune in and use the overview approach so that you can be objective. We sometimes need that adjustment most when we feel we need it least. Your countenance will reflect the good feelings you carry within.

President Gordon B. Hinckley reminded us of what we should be working toward when he said, "Cultivate an attitude of happiness. Cultivate a spirit of optimism. Walk with faith, rejoicing in the beauties of nature, in the goodness of those you love, in the testimony which you carry in your heart concerning things divine." (" 'If Thou Art Faithful,'" *Ensign*, November 1984, p. 92.)

A smile (inside and out!) brightens any face and improves anyone's image. Let's follow President Ezra Taft Benson's counsel to "live joyfully. Live happily. Live enthusiastically, knowing that God does not dwell in gloom and melancholy, but in light and love." ("Your Charge: To Increase in Wisdom and Favor with God and Man," *New Era*, September 1979, p. 42.)

Be of Good Cheer

Pointer number two: make a concerted effort to be cheerful. Turn in your scriptures to John 16:33, where the Lord himself tells us to "be of good cheer." That doesn't mean to wander around with a dopey grin on your face all the time. Even the best of us have bad days. In fact, I remember being told once that if we have a bad day once in a while we should relax and enjoy it; it means we're normal! But that doesn't give us license to be the gloom-and-doom leader of our family, our ward, or our school.

Everyone who has trouble dealing with a Pollyanna first thing in the morning, please stand up. I laugh as I type this because I *am* usually a morning person. But my babbling, chirping manner can really get on some people's nerves. They need time to wake up and get going for the day. I've watched the Pollyanna types and the Grouchy-Dwarf types interact. It's fun! Have you ever been the bubbly, bright, happy-snappy person who tried to lighten things up? Have you ever been yelled at or asked to leave because your cheer was too much to be tolerated? Hey, you could be tossed out for lots of worse things.

More power to you as you work at being the cheerleader of the crowd. Most times your efforts will really be appreciated. And you with your smiling countenance will look much more handsome than your brooding, sour counterparts! In fact, your countenance will advertise the fact that you are a loving, cheerful person.

Humility

Your life will be less complicated if you desire to let the Lord guide your path. As you give up your itinerary and give your will to God, you will be happier in your life's station. It will be much less necessary to receive the applause of the world because you will enjoy the praise of heaven, which is that good, warm feeling that you feel in the center of your being. The honors of the world won't mean as much to you, and jealousy, pride, and envy are words that will never describe you. You can relax and enjoy whatever success comes without getting big-headed. Another great thing is that you won't be upset over your friends' successes. Here are a few illustrations:

- Your best friend makes the football team, but you don't. *It's OK!*
- You wanted the lead in the school musical, but you got a part in the chorus. Bummer, because your good friend got a lead part. *It's all right!*
- You studied like a maniac to ace your geometry test and pulled a C. Lucy didn't even open her books, and she got an A-. *No problem!*
- You're on student council and seminary council, you are involved in three clubs, and you have a different date every weekend. You are grateful but don't place yourself above anybody else in your school. *Congratulations!*

You roll with the punches with a good head on your shoulders because you keep things in proper perspective. Humility plays a big part in getting to that point.

President Spencer W. Kimball once wrote these beautiful words about humility at its best:

> Humility is royalty without a crown,
> Greatness in plain clothes,
> Erudition without decoration,
> Wealth without display,
> Power without scepter or force,
> Position demanding no preferential rights,
> Greatness sitting in the congregation,
> Prayer in closets and not in corners of the street,

> Fasting in secret without publication,
> Stalwartness without a label,
> Supplication upon its knees,
> Divinity riding an ass.
> ("Humility," *Improvement Era*,
> August 1963, p. 704.)

Looking for the honors of the world will be short-lived. In true humility, we can find all the confidence we will ever need. A quiet dignity can come to us. Our willingness to learn and change will allow us a greater capacity to love and be loved without limitations.

Keep the Commandments

"Keep the commandments! In this there is safety; in this there is peace" (*Children's Songbook*, p. 146). I have loved that children's song since the first time I heard it. The only real safety and peace we will have in this world will be a result of our efforts and self-discipline to keep the commandments.

Another hymn I enjoy is "Who's on the Lord's Side?" (*Hymns*, no. 260). Well, if we take a look at the scriptures, we get a good idea of who is on the Lord's side:

> David: yes
> Goliath: no
> Joseph (of the coat of many colors): yes
> His brothers: no (but they came around later)
> Nephi: yes
> Lemuel and Laman: no (Did you ever notice how *Laman* sounds so similar to *lemon?*)
> Abel: yes
> Cain: no

We could go on for a while with that game. In fact, you might want to add some additional names to the list. Then go to the scriptures and read the entire stories involving those people. You will learn new things and gain added strength to fight your own battles and do what is right.

As much as we all want to be loved and admired, the love we should first seek to be worthy of is our Father's and his Son's. Abraham was called "the Friend of God" (James 2:23). What kind of life did Abraham live? The Abrahams of today's world are the ones who are still willing to do what it takes, placing the relationship with God above all others. It means giving up the things of the world that bring temporary pleasure but no lasting joy. It involves being true to the covenants we made at baptism. (I want to break into song here: "True to the truth for which martyrs have perished" ["True to the Faith," *Hymns*, no. 254].)

I met a young man at an Especially for Youth session where I was teaching one summer. He seemed ordinary in appearance and manner, but when I started talking with him it was clear that he was anything but ordinary. Brad had been introduced to the gospel by finding a pamphlet one day. He read it and took the initiative to call the Church for information. Missionaries were dispatched to talk with him. His family was not big on the idea of Brad studying the Mormon Church. They asked him to drop it. Brad wanted to obey his family rules, but something within him yearned to know more. Because he had been given a copy of the Book of Mormon, he read and studied it on his own. Many months passed, and he asked permission to study with the missionaries again. He was told, "No way." So Brad continued to read, study, and pray on his own. From time to time he would drive past the chapel and long to go inside. But his desire to honor his parents kept him from doing so. To be honest, there may have been a certain amount of fear that kept Brad outside the Church as well. I didn't ask any questions and Brad didn't volunteer any additional information, but I got the feeling he was afraid of his dad.

When he turned eighteen, Brad no longer needed his parent's permission to join the Church. So he visited with the local leaders, had appointments with the missionaries, and set a date to be baptized. Then he told his parents of his intentions. They went ballistic. He was told that if he joined the Mormon Church, he could kiss his family good-bye because he was no longer welcome in their home. Brad made the sacrifice most of us could not imagine. When he was baptized, his family disowned him. Now, at age eighteen and a half, Brad was at an EFY session. And what an example he was! Full of spirit and energy, he was the happiest, most self-confident person there. His attitude was positive and full of faith. He was so humble and teachable. Brad made a commitment to follow Christ. He could have been a banner boy for the theme of "keep the commandments." Clearly he *wanted* to do the right things.

I guess we could say that Rad Brad (his nickname) was a great example of pretty is as pretty does. He was not one who would be first choice in a lineup of oh-my-stars-is-he-ever-*gorgeous* guys, but you should have seen the magnet he was! The young women loved him, the young men thought he was awesome, and he was every counselor's dream participant and a role model for all the others there. He loved everybody. And he wasn't afraid to show it.

Look around you. Notice the people who seem genuinely settled in their own worth, the ones with inner beauty and integrity. They don't need to walk around with signs pinned to their shirts that read "I Win!" or "Am I good-looking or what?" (although my son Michael *does* have a T-shirt with the words "Yes, I always look this good") because their face and their manner reflect the beauty within them. It is obvious that they love the world and the people in it. They are happy. They make *us* feel happier. Let's go and do likewise, without limitations!

A Few Things You Can Do

- Sing "Don't worry; be happy" until you feel that way.
- Clear up any misunderstandings with friends, the sooner the better.

- Next time you're in the car, wave and smile at passersby.
- Say something loving to your little brother or sister, even if they really are getting on your nerves (your parents may be very surprised by this gesture).
- If you start to judge someone, think of the bag lady and repent right then and there! (That's what I do.)
- Look for something good in every single person you see today.
- Pray for the Lord's direction in becoming a more loving, pretty-on-the-inside person.

9

Standards: Where Do You Stand?

Choose you this day whom ye will serve.
—Joshua 24:15

When I was a little girl I watched shows such as *Leave It To Beaver.* The Beave's family was an average, two-parent one. The mom always dressed up (in dress and pearls, no less), and her house was in perfect order. The parents worked out (quite easily) their differences between each other and the children. Mom and Dad slept in twin beds. Mom and Dad were never inappropriate in their speech or manner.

I wonder what Beaver's family would be like today? Unlike the shows of long ago, twin beds are never even seen on television. Sex is shown as casual and normal with or without a serious, loving relationship. If problems are ever settled, it is often with the assistance of therapists or guns. Very little is left to the imagination with regard to the human body. Tops cut down to here and dresses hiked up to there are the norm. Language is reprehensible. For every slight imaginable, the answer seems to be "Sue the jerk!" and the attorneys are brought in. It makes me tired just thinking about it!

The following words by Elder Joseph B. Wirthlin of the Quorum of the Twelve Apostles are absolutely awesome: "Just forty years ago, President J. Reuben Clark, Jr., a member of the First Presidency, gave an address titled 'Slipping from Our Old Moorings.' He described how we have slipped away from living the Ten Commandments (see *Church News,* 8 March 1947, pp. 1, 8–9). If we had slipped away then, where are we forty years later? In 1947, television and computers were in their infancies. We had no satellite broadcasts or videotapes and no computer fraud. Certainly our moral standards of decency and propriety have slipped from where they were in 1947. The obscenity, nudity, and other forms of pornography that would have made us blush and turn away in shame in 1947 are now thrust at us openly in printed and audiovisual material. They are even paraded through our homes unless we are careful to keep them out. As a people, we are slipping further from our old moorings today because we are not following our prophets." ("Patience, a Key to Happiness," *Ensign*, May 1987, p. 30.)

May 1987! That was over a decade ago. How much have standards declined even in the last decade? Indeed, we all probably agree with President Hinckley, who quoted Ted Koppel as saying, "What Moses brought down from Mount Sinai were not The Ten Suggestions" (In "Our Solemn Responsibilities," *Ensign*, November 1991, p. 51).

We live in a different world, my young friends. More is required of you than was required of your parents or grandparents. In order to stay afloat in this sea of spiritual mud, you have to identify your standards and stick to them. You will be identifiable by those standards. And, being desirous of returning to our heavenly home, you want to make sure your standards are proper and worthy ones. The old-fashioned values and standards are the ones chosen by followers of Christ. Those old values are not chosen because there is a comfort zone in choosing the old ways but because "through the ages they have proved right" (Spencer W. Kimball, "President Kimball Speaks Out on Morality," *Ensign*, November 1980, p. 96).

In a newfangled world, how do we hold on to the old-fashioned standards without seeming out of step with the world? How do we hold up our light without getting burned? And how do we find the right friends and associates, ones who believe and act like we do?

It is time to make our stand and stand firm. President Spencer W. Kimball said we should "make certain decisions only once. . . . We can make a single decision about certain things that we will incorporate in our lives and then make them ours—without having to brood and redecide a hundred times what it is we will do and what we will not do." ("Boys Need Heroes Close By," *Ensign,* May 1976, p. 46.)

We have been given the honorable responsibility to choose. I have always felt that because we have the *right to choose* we should *choose the right.* We know that CTR stands for choose the right. We know that BYU stands for Brigham Young University and FBI stands for Federal Bureau of Investigation. The temple stands for heavenly things such as purity, eternal covenants, peace, celestial teachings. What do *you* stand for? And what do you stand *against?* If we are to be strong and immovable in the Lord's kingdom, it is necessary to take the time to figure out what matters most. Then we can align our actions with our proper thoughts. We can decide once and for all what we will and will not do and say. People will know us by our actions. Even though they might disagree, they will respect us for standing our ground. And they might learn a whole lot from our example.

There were once three young Jewish guys who were good friends and good followers of the Lord. They were determined to stand firm for the things they believed. The community leader told them to knock it off with their worship thing, that they had to listen up to the things *he* said and do the things everybody else was doing. The three refused. The big shot gave them a chance to give up their practices and stop acting so holier-than-thou or else he would make sure they felt the heat. Literally. The three young Jewish fellows are known as Shadrach, Meshach, and Abed-nego. Their story is told in the Old Testament in the book called Daniel. If you will open your scriptures to the third chapter, you can read the entire tale of those three amazing young men. King Nebuchadnezzar is the big shot in the story who ordered the young men sent to the fire. Read of how the heat was so intense that the king's attendants were consumed! Note how the king was told that the three were walking within the furnace and that there seemed to be a fourth with them! What an amazing testimony of strength and courage the young men carried with them. And what a blessing to know that the Lord does walk with us through our fires of affliction. Don't you wonder about the details surrounding Shadrach and company *after* their ordeal? We do know that the king was impressed enough to make sure no one should speak against their God and that they were promoted in the kingdom.

There are times when we are called to walk through our fires of adversity. We may or may not have others to stand with us. But stand we must. As surely as Shadrach, Meshach and Abed-nego were attended by the Lord shall we feel his help. We may get singed and we might have to wait awhile for everything to come out in the wash, but all will be made right. We will feel good about ourselves for doing what our hearts tell us is true, and we will make a statement that will attract those who appreciate our standards.

Just as King Nebuchadnezzar had standards which were far removed from those of the three friends, so our society has very different standards than those the Lord has set for us. Let's examine just a few so that you can make sure you stand on solid ground.

Entertainment

We have been counseled to stay away from R-rated movies. Some of them have great stories or are beautifully made with just one or two bad parts. In a national poll taken in 1992, teenagers aged sixteen and under all across the U.S. were asked if they had seen an R-rated movie in the last year. The percentage of those who had slipped into at least one R-rated movie was a resounding ninety-six percent. Then a poll was taken of active, seminary-attending Latter-day Saint teenagers. The percentage of those who had seen an R-rated movie in the past year? Roughly ninety-one percent! What is wrong with this picture? Many use the argument that PG-13 movies, or even PG movies, are "just as bad or worse." It seems a simple decision to stay away from *any* offensive media. Anything that influences us in a negative way, that robs us of the Spirit, can and should be avoided! Is seeing that movie (the one that everyone is talking about) with the "one or two bad parts" really worth bruising your spirit over? Nah!

A father who wanted to teach the importance of not falling for the only-one-bad-part syndrome chose an interesting way of making his point. For family home evening the mother reminded everyone of the standards set forth for us and talked of choices. Defenses came to the surface and there were a couple of problems with everyone seeing eye to eye, but they enjoyed the lively discussion. Afterwards Dad went into the kitchen to make his famous milk shakes for dessert. The kids loved those milk shakes. Dad was up there with the best when it came to his ice-cream concoctions. With three blenders out and all ingredients in the holders, Dad dropped a big, fat, juicy (and dead) fly into each blender. You can imagine the faces of the children as they watched their father ruin three perfectly good containers of their favorite shakes! As Dad hit the button he looked at his children and said, "Hey, there's only one bad part. All the rest is awesome!" The kids got the point. So did I when I heard the story. Only one bad part is not healthy; it contaminates and messes up the rest. Choosing to attend a good movie with one bad part can be more unhealthy than we imagine. *Where do you stand?*

Dress Standards

What about dress standards? What does your style of dress say about your character? Many times I hear comments such as "It's my life; I can dress however I want" or "No one should judge me if my clothes and hair are different." Indeed, that is true. But people do make value judgments. What does your style of clothing and hair say about you? If you are sending mixed messages, it would be just fine to drop the pretense of rebel and dress as you would if you were going to see the Savior.

When young men and women are in jeans or shorts, they are more casual in manner. When guys put on their shirt and tie and girls put on dresses or skirts, their actions are more refined for the most part. Both types of dress are totally acceptable, and I feel sure the Lord will be as comfortable with us in our casual wear as our Sunday best. But when people enter the chapel in good Sunday dress, they are more likely to behave in a reverent manner. And if we choose to wear tight, revealing clothes or outlandish things that seem edgier and more worldly, the chances are we will *feel* that way too.

Girls, if you have gone shopping for a prom or other dressy occasion, you have probably been disappointed with the choices available. The dresses are way too short or the necklines plunge to your knees. It is frustrating. Often we end up buying a dress and adding material here and there to make it work. I agree with what my good friend Steven K. Perry said: "We used to live in an age of strapless evening gowns. Now we live in a world of gownless evening straps!" Ha! Isn't it true? It is hard to fit in and yet conform to the Lord's standards. But the Lord's standards they are.

If you are a young man reading this book, does your eye stray to the young woman wearing short shorts and a halter top, leaving little to the imagination? Maybe. Would you be happy if when you are one day married your wife chose to dress that way? I don't think so. To be real and strong, we have to walk the walk as well as talk the talk. Now is the time to decide what is and is not appropriate as far as dress is concerned. We can help each other in that course of action. We want to surround ourselves with friends who make it easier to do what we know is best. *Where do you stand?*

Dating

You know these answers: How old are we supposed to be when we start dating? _____ Steady dating? _____ What kind of conduct is appropriate when we are dating? _____

_____

We have been told we should begin dating at age sixteen, not age fifteen and ten months. Some interesting statistics have been gathered on this subject:

- If a person starts dating at age twelve or thirteen (which is prevalent in our society as a whole), the chances of having a problem with morality are 86 percent.
- If a person starts dating at age sixteen (which LDS standards reinforce), the chances of having problems with morality are 18 percent.
- If a person steady dates, the chances of committing a moral sin increase by 121 percent!

Can you see why the prophet has given us certain guidelines? If we want to be safe, then we have to wear the life vest of certain standards! *Where do you stand?*

Regardless of what area of conduct we are dealing with, conforming to the Lord's standards will keep us safe and allow us to have the companionship of the Holy Ghost. We will be able to feel the Spirit's direction as to whom we should associate with and what we should get involved in. We will have fewer furnaces of affliction to walk through if we are staying on the strait and narrow.

For years I have been haunted by the need some young people have to fit in at any cost. More than a decade ago I started a song based on the need to stand up and be counted so that we aren't deceived. Following is the lyrical part of the finished product of that song "Stand or Fall" I started so many years ago. My collaborative partner Randy Kartchner and I produced it for a Bookcraft album in 1997.

Stand or Fall

You better stand for something
Or you might fall for anything.
So you have to live your life before a judge and jury,
But do you have to worry?

Linda loves the little things that matter in life.
She gets 'em any way she can, and she pays the price.
Wanda always worries 'bout the way she's perceived.
The things the TV tells her are the things she believes.

Tommy totes a gun, he says he's got to be safe.
If pushin' comes to shove he'll hold it right in your face.
Mary may be pretty but she's hidin' behind
The twenty tons of makeup baby—she must be blind!

Don't it always sound like Donald's singin' the blues?
Seems like what he's needin' is a new attitude.
Connie won't be caught without a man at her side
Thinks she isn't something if she's not with a guy.

You better stand for something
Or you might fall for anything!
("Just Be Yourself" [Salt Lake City: Bookcraft, 1997],
Vickey Pahnke/Randy Kartchner.)

    As the world gets dimmer, we have to shine brighter and stand taller. Navigating through temptations and difficulties at school or at work can be tough. Knowing and living the standards the Lord has set can get you through the rough spots, and allow you to be the example a friend or co-worker is needing. We have the gospel with all its principles and direction to help us live what we know is right! It's time to stand up and be counted!

    Aristotle, whose name is synonymous with knowledge and wisdom to many, observed that "we become brave by doing brave acts" (from Aristotle's *Nicomachean Ethics*. In William Bennett, *The Book of Virtues* [New York: Simon and Shuster], p. 441).

    I love that thought! Although there is much pollution in this world, there is an army of young, strong warriors who are willing to take upon themselves the name of Christ and advertise it! You are one of them. As you live the standards you know are correct, your influence is noted by many silent observers.

If you ever feel overwhelmed (and who doesn't from time to time?) and unsure of how to handle the obstacle in front of you, try to remember that "the task ahead of us is never as great as the power behind us." That quote is actually attributed to the Alcoholics Anonymous program. Those who join the program do not advertise their resolves. But their determination is so great that you can almost see the flashing sign on their forehead that says, "I can overcome!" Build relationships with those who dare to advertise their religion by living it. Strengthen your own testimony of things that count by sharing with others who love the Lord and are willing to pay the price. Whatever fiery furnaces you are called to go through will be easier to handle if you are surrounded by people who are willing to "take upon you the name of Christ" (Mormon 8:38).

Ardeth G. Kapp has shared these insightful words about the importance of pulling together to keep our direction steady: "Standards of the Church have been given to us to protect us and to help us grow spiritually. When the pioneers ended a day's journey, each night they checked their wagons for any needed repairs. They united in prayer for continued guidance and protection and took a reading of both distance and direction to see how far they had traveled and make sure they were on the right trail. We would do well to follow the same pattern today. A good measurement to ask concerning every important decision is whether or not this decision will move you toward or away from making and keeping sacred covenants and preparing for the ordinances of the temple." ("'Crickets' Can Be Destroyed through Spirituality," *Ensign*, November 1990, p. 95.)

In other words, my dear friends, the tests and challenges we face are the decisions between good and evil. Not wealth or lack of it, not fame or obscurity, not being part of the in crowd or being a social outcast by virtue of not following the current leader's ideas of what is in. Television's and the world's standards may have reached the bottom, but the gospel standards are immovable. Where do you stand? Once you have clearly defined that answer in your own mind and heart, you are likely to seek out those who feel the same. Remember, since we have the right to choose we should choose the right! We *can* hold up our light without getting burned or without having it snuffed out in a dark world. God bless you as you take your stand and make a difference for good!

A Few Things You Can Do

- Get rid of your CDs and tapes that don't conform to standards. Today!
- Determine your decisions concerning certain things right now, and let it be settled.
- Toss out your tight-fitting tops or other questionable clothing.
- Pray for help in living the standards you know are correct.
- Talk with someone who is struggling with these kinds of issues; you will both be better for the conversation that reinforces proper choices.
- Wear a CTR ring every day and remember what it is for!
- Think, *What would I do differently if the Savior were here?*
- Study the words of the prophets concerning right and wrong choices.

10

Birds of a Feather

*Iron sharpeneth iron;
so a man sharpeneth the countenance of his friend.*
—Proverbs 27:17

Who are your friends? And how do you know? Do they bring out the best in you? Are they there for you when you need them? Have you ever been burned by someone you thought you could trust? What are friends for, anyway? How do we connect, grow, and build great relationships?

Life can be a lot easier when we have friends to share with us, cry with us, laugh with us, and assure us that we are OK, even when we make mistakes.

My daughter once said to me, "Mom, I'm so embarrassed I could just die! I'll never be able to show my face in public again!" I told her, "Honey, embarrassing moments run in our family. Your friends know to expect such things from us. And, Andrea, if a person could die from embarrassment, I would have been dead a long time ago."

You need to understand that my life has been a series of humiliating incidents. They make great stories now, but at the time I have wanted to crawl in a hole and stay there. Can you relate? When I first came to Utah as a student at BYU I decided I would leave the old me at home in Virginia and start anew. What a great plan! I would make new friends, and no one would know I was the klutz of the East Coast! That was flawed thinking; I failed to realize that I was bringing *myself* with me. Let me illustrate.

Early in the year I saw this nice-looking guy at sacrament meeting, a returned missionary. He seemed to have credibility because he was the ward clerk. (Whatever.) It seemed a healthy goal to want to date a lot of different guys, and this one seemed a good choice for my dating journal. I pulled out my mental checklist, and he did very well. Young men, you need to know that girls *do* have checklists. And they send their friends to do background checks on you so that they know more about you than you might imagine!

Anyway, he was cute; check. He was an RM; check. He smiled and could carry on a decent conversation (I watched him do so with other ward members and observed from afar); check. I wondered what I could do to catch his eye. I was in luck! As a member of our ward Relief Society presidency, I had been asked to speak in church the following Sunday. I knew what to do! This guy was so newly home from his mission that his halo was still glowing atop his head; here was my chance to prepare diligently, deliver sweetly, and blow him away with my spirituality! (I know my reasoning left something to be desired.) On Sunday, as I stood at the podium I looked down in the front row to see the object of my preparation grinning up at me. As I began my remarks, we exchanged smiles. From time to time I would glance at him, and he continued to flash a genuine, full-toothed, happy face. I thought, *Yes! This is working! He wants to know who I am!*

I concluded, and as I began walking confidently down the steps that would take me directly past him to my seat, the heel broke on my shoe. I slid down the steps and sprawled at the feet of the young ward clerk. Agghh! The truth was out! Now the entire ward knew the real Vickey; I was as accident-prone in Utah as I had been in Virginia. I was so embarrassed I wanted to walk out of the building and never come back. It didn't take long for everyone to learn that if they wanted to have fun they should hang around me because *something* would happen that would make them laugh.

Shortly thereafter we decided as a ward to go roller skating. What a blast this would be! It was something I had never done before! At that time I had very long hair, which could be a pain to wash and style every day. For the outing I decided to pull my hair up, pin it with a zillion hairpins, and wear a wig.

Bad plan. As the others skated with great abandon, I clung to the railing for dear life. But gradually, with confidence growing, I let go and picked up a little speed. This was fun! This was awesome! I could do it!

In life, as we become more comfortable with things, our confidence grows. As we work at something, it becomes easier and we do a better job. So it seemed with this skating experience. I let go of the railing and started around the rink. I had not realized that at one spot, a little further out from the safety rail, the flooring did not quite come together evenly. As I skated along, increasing in confidence and pace, I hit that uneven flooring. My feet flew out from under me, I landed on my backside, and the wig flew off my head.

The whole place came to a standstill. Everyone seemed to simultaneously stifle a gasp or a laugh. The fellow who skates around to keep order came to me, picked up my wig, and asked, "Does this belong to you?" I was so embarrassed I thought I would die. But I didn't; I merely provided another good laugh for my friends.

Those guys proved they really were friends because they stuck with me. Through many episodes like that I learned an important lesson about my new associates: they accepted me for who I was. What a blessing to feel loved and cared about even with my obvious imperfections. Because of their acceptance, my friends helped me to better accept myself. I learned that friends make it easier to get back up after we've fallen down (do you have your spiritual ears on here?) and to start over again. *If* we choose the right friends, they will love us and help us learn to better love ourselves. Good friends make all the difference in the quality of life we enjoy.

What are some traits you consider important for

good friendships? List five things that are essential to having or being a true friend:

_____

_____

_____

_____

_____

Learning to cultivate true friendships is so important. We aren't meant to make it through our earthly journey alone. Heavenly Father often answers our prayers through those we are close to. They are the ones who quietly whisper encouragement or sternly admonish us with warnings for our good. We *need* friends. Even the Savior surrounded himself with those he called friends.

We need to learn to discern true friends from false ones and to be a true friend to others. How are you at spotting a real friend from a phony? Let me share with you a few prototype friends. You decide whether someone you know fits this description. You might even want to ponder whether you could be identified with one of our role models in some way.

First, there is Holly. Holly is a role player. She must be in at all costs. She seems confident and sure of herself but secretly seeks approval through sporting the right labels on her clothing, the current cool hair style, or the latest hot fad. If you want to be her friend, *you* must have those things too. Otherwise she can't afford to take a chance on hanging out with a nobody. It would look bad for her!

Then there is Polly. You *have* what she *wants*. She is your best friend as long as there is something in it for her. When her need for what you supply is gone, so is she. Here is an illustration: You are the new kid in town. It just so happens that your dad makes a lot of money. You live in big house with a pool, tennis courts, the whole works. You are flattered when Polly latches on to you and makes you her friend. Shortly after your friendship begins, Polly has a great idea: there can be a big party! At your house! They can use your house, your food, your pool—use *you.* When the party is over, so is the friendship. Have you ever known anyone like Polly?

Molly is our third type of so-called friend. Have you ever heard the term *Molly Mormon?* That term does not fit *this* Molly. Our Molly is a flake, but you can't help but like her even though she cancels out on you at the last minute (when something better comes along). She doesn't know what the words *follow through* even mean, but she is such a flatterer that you just have to let her off the hook time and time again. Does the word *shallow* fit here?

Our next friend Dolly dares you. If *she* is going to be involved in something on the edge, so should you. You might be tempted to say or do things in her company that you wouldn't dream of otherwise. "Misery loves company" is a phrase that comes to mind. After all, if she takes a fall she wants you coming down with her. Or she might just need a scapegoat; that's where you come in handy. How many Dollys have you known?

Finally, there is Lolly. She is the one who dumps all her woes on you. Every day brings a new emergency that you have to help fix. She would love to help you sometime, but she's always up to her neck in her own crisis of the moment. If relationships are a two-way street, Lolly definitely lives on a one-way road.

Are there any changes you need to make in your circle of friends or in your own attitude? With careful consideration, you might find you have been wasting time on relationships that can go nowhere. Cultivating true friendships based on Christlike principles will make it easier to love yourself and love the gospel. If birds of a feather flock together, you will want to fly with the best of the flock!

Can you imagine Moroni's sadness when he wrote, "I have not friends nor whither to go" (Mormon 8:5). My heart hurts for him at that point in his life. We need friendships to build on now and enjoy forever. Although I have often missed the mark, I would like to share with you a few thoughts on building better relationships with friends.

Love Yourself

You have heard this tons of times. But I include it because we really *can't* open our hearts and love other people until we understand how important it is to love ourselves. Not the prideful, me-first love or the when-I-look-in-the-mirror-I-am-amazed-at-how-wonderful-I-am love. Just a comfortable acceptance of who we are and what we can become. If "the only way to have a friend is to be one" (Ralph Waldo Emerson), let's first be good to ourselves. From that sturdy foundation of self-acceptance, we will be able to choose better friends and be a better one. Check the scripture in D&C 38:24. Mark the thought that a friend should "esteem his brother as himself."

Be Positive

Here's an experiment to try: Just for one day, vow to think only positive thoughts about yourself and everybody else. If criticisms creep in, chase them away like you would the plague. You will have to go twenty-four hours and not complain about one single thing, not the weather, your homework, your hair, a job that needs doing, or the fact that your ears flop in the wind. Nothing but positive output! Your desire to be positive will be a magnet for your friends. They might wonder if you're sick or something, but maybe they'll join in and you can support one another in this twenty-four hour challenge! St. Francis of Assisi once remarked, "A single sunbeam is enough to drive away many shadows." Awesome thought! And true!

Share Your Emotions

I've noticed that some people have a hard time sharing things that are tender. Our society tends to make it difficult to share the whole spectrum of our feelings without being uncomfortable. That's sad, because better friendships come from being more open. One dear friend of mine, a wonderful person loaded with talent, fun, and sensitivity, used to find it difficult to show his tears. Once, while recording an album, a group of us decided to go see the movie *Dead Poets Society*. Remember the very most intense part of that movie, when you wanted to bawl? Well, I *was*. Tears were falling freely (it was great) when my friend leaned over and whispered in my ear, "Hi! I'm Batman!" I turned to see him grinning, and I just wanted to kick him! He had ruined my moment! To break the tension and save himself from the tears that were about to leak, he resorted to his own brand of humor. It saved him from crying. And we laughed about the incident for a long time.

Randy is now married with children of his own. It is easy and comfortable for him to share the more vulnerable side of himself at this stage of our friendship. We have discussed how holding in those feelings that are best expressed can deny some extra blessings of closer friendship. True friends share both happy and sad times, knowing that strength comes from sharing. I guess we could say birds of a feather understand the importance of sharing!

Enjoy the Gift of Laughter

Having already talked about the importance of having a sense of humor, let's just review how important laughter can be in improving our friendships. There is an old saying that goes, "He who laughs, lasts!" Whoever penned those words goes by the name Anonymous, so we don't know who to thank for the insight. But there is no denying that a healthy dose of laughter thrown into the mix can help even the best of relationships.

J. Golden Kimball was a leader known for, among other things, his quick wit. I love the story of how he turned a really bad situation around with this gift:

He was serving a mission in the southern states and was assigned to enter an area where missionary work had been shut down because of some real problems. There was a minister of another faith who hated the Mormons and made things so difficult that the work could not progress. Elder Kimball must have been nervous to return to that unfriendly area. He and his companion were out knocking on doors their very first day when they came to the house that would change everything. When Elder Kimball knocked, who do you suppose came to the door? Yes, the minister. He was a great big man with an imposing physique. With a slow, sly grin he put out his hand to Elder Kimball and said, "Well, good morning, sons of the devil." Agghh! Can you imagine? I probably would have turned and headed for the hills. Not J. Golden. Thinking quickly, he put his hand out and with a smile answered, "Well, good morning, father!" Now *that* was quick thinking. And do you know what? The minister laughed and invited the two young elders into his home. They built bridges of friendship and tore down those walls of hate and hurt.

As is so often the case, that minister was a fine man. He just had not understood what the missionaries were about. He had not known the right information about the Church. That man and the elders became friends. The work progressed, all because one person used the gift of humor well!

If, as Victor Hugo once remarked, "laughter is the sun that drives winter from the human face," shouldn't we be involved in warming things up? I would venture to say that what it does for the human face it does in triplicate for the heart!

Practice Makes Perfect

We might be amazed how we are able to cultivate better friendships by practicing on a daily basis, even when we are in a lousy mood and don't feel like being nice. The little things certainly do count. When we wake up in a bad mood, we take it out on, yes, the family. Because, after all, they will love us *anyway*. Some homes are close to ideal and others are far from it, but there is always room for improvement in how we treat our family. Doing better within the walls of our homes seems to magically improve our relationships outside our family. Anyway, these people are our forever friends. It was from a friend I'll call Tina that I learned the importance of practicing kindness at home so that we don't live with regrets.

Tina is an average person with good days and bad ones. On a Saturday years back, she awoke in a *bad* mood. Stomping downstairs, she announced that she would not be going on the family picnic as planned. Tina's family knew her well enough that they knew it was going to be hard to turn that mood around. But they tried. Mom gave her a hug and asked her to reconsider. No way. Dad tried to make her laugh and turn her around, but Tina would have no part of it. Her brothers told her she was going to miss a good day at the beach and tried to talk her into it. Then her little sister, just learning to talk and toddling about, came over to her, looked up into Tina's face, and said, "Tina go wif us? I wuv Tina." Oooh, that got her right in the heart. But there was a principle involved here. She was *mad*, and she was going to enjoy it! She would not be going on their picnic, period!

Reluctantly Mom and Dad, brothers, and little sister packed the car and gave Tina hugs or a wave before happily driving off for their day at the beach, leaving their sulking family member at home. Tina did not see them again. On the way to the beach, their car collided with another, killing them all.

I share that story only so that you may think about the way you treat your family, even when you're in a bad mood or need to take it out on someone. We will never regret sharing loving, happy times. "A friend loveth at all times" (Proverbs 17:17), even on bad days. Even when we don't feel like it!

Focus on Your Truest Friend

A line of scripture reminds us that "thy friends do stand by thee" (D&C 121:9). It is during moments of great need that our truest friend always stands by us. Focusing on Christ and trying to love as he loves is our surest way of being and finding the right friend. There will be times of despair and heartache for all of us. At those difficult times we find our faith increases and our loving friendship with the Savior grows as we learn to know and trust him. In fact, no one else, regardless of how much they love us, can help us like the Savior can.

As I share three little stories of how the Lord's caring made all the difference, you may recall other stories you have heard and how they caused your own faith to grow.

The first is about a little girl who was diagnosed with a fatal kidney ailment. She had spent weeks in the hospital only to have one kidney fail and the other quickly deteriorate. The doctors finally told the child's parents they should take her home so that her last few days could be spent in the comfort of her own house.

The child had been taught to pray, and the story goes that she balled her little hands into fists and fervently prayed aloud that Heavenly Father would heal her and allow her to live. Her weak little voice could be heard up and down the corridor of the pediatric wing. The next day she was taken home to die. Several days passed, and the little one seemed much better. The next week, doing much better, she was taken in to see the doctor. After examination and testing, the treating doctor shook his head and said, "If I hadn't treated her myself, I wouldn't believe it. She has two functioning kidneys. You may take your little girl home. She's going to be just fine." The child learned at an early age that she had a true friend, one in whom she could trust.

The second story is of a young married woman who was eager to be a mother. After a couple of devastating miscarriages, she was privileged once again to carry a child. Several months into the pregnancy she fell ill. The doctor who had seen her through her previous difficulties gently took her hand and explained that she had HELLP syndrome, which usually takes the life of the baby and of the mother as well. She was shattered.

Shortly thereafter, the young woman was given a blessing in which she was told that if she would trust in her truest friend he would watch over her and all would be well. Several months later she gave birth to a healthy baby girl. Mother and daughter were fine. The young woman learned who she could trust, and she understood the importance of accepting the Lord's loving guidance.

Now let me tell you of a woman busy with family, church, and community work. She seemed to have a charmed life until she began experiencing head pain and ear and equilibrium problems. The first doctor she visited sent her to another, who sent her to another. After preliminary tests were run, the doctor bluntly told the woman that she had either a certain disease or a brain tumor. A CT scan was run to determine the answer. When the results came back, the CT scan was positive for a tumor on the right side of the brain. It appeared inoperable.

The woman lost it for a while. What would become of her family? Why was this happening? Despair clouded her judgment and attitude. After a while she received a priesthood blessing that told her the Lord loved her and was mindful of her. If she would exercise sufficient faith, all would be well. A repeat CT scan was done a short time later. Where there had been a tumor, there was a blank space on the right side of the head! The woman learned whom she could trust. Her faith grew stronger, and she understood a little more about true friendship and comfort for the soul.

Those stories are sacred to me, my young brothers and sisters. Some of you may know that I was that little girl. It was my parents who were told to take me home to die. I was that young woman who so desperately wanted a baby. The child born to me is my daughter Andrea, now a vibrant and beautiful young lady herself. And I was that busy mother who fell ill. I have seen the CT scan reports that show where a tumor was evident. I have seen the reports that now show a blank space. Actually, I use it as an excuse from time to time: "What do you expect? I have a blank space in my head!"

Having been there and done that, I *know* from my own experience that although there are friends who would do anything for us during difficult times, no one can provide the uplift and assurance we need except our very truest friend. Trust me on this.

I have come to learn how much I must depend on the Lord and how truly loving he is. I have witnessed how he is there for us when no one else can salve our hurting bodies and burdened hearts. Indeed, we may be "healed by the power of the Lamb of God" (1 Nephi 11:31).

Those personal experiences are ones I share a little hesitantly, but I want you to know that no matter what crisis you are called to go through, the Lord will be at your side! I want you to know, dear friend reading this right now, that there are many who have more faith than I have. There are many more educated in the gospel and much better than I. You are probably such a person. If you have prayed with all the fervor of your soul and your prayer seems unanswered, realize that Heavenly Father loves you enough to give you what you *need*. That might be very different from what you *want*.

There have been times when I have petitioned heaven for a certain cause or blessing and I have had to say good-bye to loved ones or I have had to let go of a dream, a heart's desire, or a goal that was not in keeping with Father's will, at least not in my time frame. Our truest friend knows what is best for us. He will make sure we are taken care of with "every needful thing" (D&C 88:119). We only need to trust.

Sometimes during my not-so-noble moments I am quietly reminded of my friend's sacrifice for me, of his loving assistance, and of his desire to have me likewise be a true friend to others. If birds of a feather flock together, let's make sure *we* are part of the Savior's flock. He will be there during the times we need him most. He will help us get along better with our family. His influence will allow us to use the great gift of laughter in a heavenly way. His love allows us to be more open with our feelings. His Spirit allows us to be more positive.

When we share the most important yet simple elements of friendship, the other elements seem to fall into place. Good, eternal relationships begin with the simplest of tools. God bless us as we practice making the best relationships, ones that will last forever!

A Few Things You Can Do

- Go tell a family member you love them right now!
- Choose one trait you want to improve upon in order to be a better friend.
- Make adjustments if some friends aren't what they're cracked up to be.
- Put a plus sign on your hand and take the twenty-four-hour challenge.
- If you blow the challenge, start over again and again!
- Pray for insight regarding your friendships.
- Learn something new about your truest friend every single day.
- Make someone laugh; it will make their day!
- Practice, practice, practice in your family!

11

Moonlight and Roses: Romance or Not?

*Set your affection on things above,
not on things on the earth.*
—*Colossians 3:2*

The beginning of the like-to-love process is a natural high. Actually, it is more of a love-to-love process. We move from loving the person as a friend to loving that person in a more romantic way. Oh, it can be glorious! But is it real? From the time that we passed notes in elementary school with messages such as, "I like you. Do you like me? Check yes or no," we have been learning to relate to people. In an effort to boost the morale of friends and budding romantic couples everywhere, here are some pointers for liking, loving, and learning to tell the difference.

We all know about the ploys used to meet a member of the opposite sex. You walk into the dance and see her across a crowded room. You want to get her attention. In doing so, you do not wish to make an idiot of yourself. You think, *Maybe if I concentrate on her hard enough, she will look my way.* She does!

> Step one is: Your eyes meet.
> Step two is: You smile at each other.
> Step three is: Taking a deep breath and walking up to her to introduce yourself.

Just so you may save yourself some trouble, let me interject here that girls cannot stand pickup lines. Remember the beauties like "Do your feet hurt? You were running through my dreams all last night" or "Do you have a quarter? My mom told me to call home when I met the girl of my dreams!" Puhleeze! Do yourself a favor and stick to real, honest-to-goodness conversation.

Once you have completed the meeting part of this relationship, you are ready to move on to the getting-to-know-you part. The secret here is to ask questions. Almost everybody likes to talk about themselves, even those shy ones who don't talk very much. Once you find out what kind of things they are interested in, you keep asking questions and making great comments, such as, "Ahhh!" "Oh, really?" and "That's cool!" If you keep smiling and keep at it, you will start a real spark for a relationship.

You two really hit it off, and you decide you want to ask her out. You do so, and again she says yes! You become friends. You share common interests, enjoy some of the same things, and can easily talk with each other. When you have gone out several times, you are sitting next to her in the movie theater and you think, *I would like very much to put my arm around this girl.* We are all aware of the guy-stretches-arms-in-mock-yawning move to let the arm fall, conveniently, around the shoulder of the girl in question. I would like to be a fly on the wall sometime, though. I've heard too many stories of how the guy feels once his arm is in the around-her-shoulder position. Ten minutes later he's thinking to himself, *My arm! It's tingly and cold and feels half-dead! What am I going to do?* Ah, the trials of dating!

Some of us may not be aware of the similar I-would-like-very-much-to-hold-this-guy's-hand ploy. Here is how it goes: A girl and guy are walking along together. The girl swings her arms loosely, slowly at her sides, very close to the boy in question. Eventually the guy's hand hits against the girl's hand. The girl has conveniently turned her hand so that it can fit very nicely into the clutch of the guy's. Since there is an extra hand in close proximity, the guy thinks, *Hmm, there is an extra hand here. I think I will hold it.*

Young woman is successful in her ploy. Young man is content. All is well in the world. Until one or the other decides there could be more to their relationship. Going out often is not enough. It is time to proclaim that they belong to each other. At this point, they should go steady. It is a popular thing to do in our culture. But it's not healthy.

Haven't you noticed that some people treat their steadies like private property? If their steady looks at another person, it is a big no-no? There is a what's-in-it-for-me? attitude. It sometimes becomes a What-*more*-is-in-it-for-me? attitude. It ends up confusing some important issues, such as am I in *like*, in *love*, or in *lust*? Eliminate the steady thing and keep your life less complicated. Yes, it may be hard. No, it won't necessarily get you more dates (although many times it does!). Yes, you *will* have fewer temptations with moral issues. You are footloose and fancy-free, as the saying goes. Enjoy it! Figure out who *you* are, what kind of person you want to be, what kind of person you want to spend forever with, and what things are and are not acceptable to you. You have years to get that all together. Rushing the issues brings misery. Count on it.

Too many times I have visited with young girls torn apart because they did something they thought they would never do or because their heart has been broken by a fellow who earlier said he loved them or because they did the unthinkable and had an abortion. They would do *anything* to turn the clock back and start over. I realize I am speaking plainly here. There is no other way if we want to talk heart to heart about serious and important issues.

Likewise, I've visited with devastated young men who have to seriously repent before going into the Missionary Training Center because of various problems they wished they had avoided altogether, at all costs.

Every time there has been a problem, it is because of misplaced loyalty or misguided feelings. Elder Robert L. Backman of the Seventy had this to say about keeping our relationships proper and aboveboard: "Keep your life clean—in thought and action. Immorality is Satan's most potent tool against us and leads to more unhappiness, grief, regret, and self-degradation than any other sin. It is deadly to our eternal progress. Avoid it like a plague." ("'Called to Serve,'" *Ensign*, November 1987, p. 62.)

For an honest story on the rewards of chastity, read in Genesis, the thirty-ninth chapter, about Joseph. That poor guy had his share of lumps, one of which was being falsely accused of trying to seduce Potiphar's wife. (Check out verses seven through twenty.) He stood true in the most dire of temptations. Eventually he was favored to become the progenitor of the two most elect tribes in Israel.

At the opposite end of the pole is the story of David. That same David who through faith and courage slew Goliath and was known and loved as a leader after the Lord's way later yielded to temptation. Open your scriptures to 2 Samuel, the eleventh chapter. You'll want to read this word for word before going forward in this book. The consequences of David's sins are heartbreaking for so many people in that story. And David lost his salvation.

Be careful, my young friends. The difference between liking or loving and lusting is vast. Although the gospel's teachings speak of us loving everyone, let's take a specific look at the girl and guy feelings of *liking* versus *loving*.

"Mingle, mingle, mingle, *seven!*" Brad Wilcox and I were teaching together at a youth conference. It was games time, and our first activity was the mingle game, a hilarious undertaking in which all the participants wander around until a number is called out and you have to make a group of that number of people. Once you're sure your group has the correct number of participants, you sit down quickly. By doing so you stay in the game. If it sounds geeky, it's just because you haven't played it. It's a riot for everybody who gets involved.

I had seen the young woman when we first got to the stake center. At game time I noticed how she hung around this certain young man, hoping he would notice her. Whether Brad called for groups of ten or three, she was right in there claiming her place close to this boy. During other parts of the conference, she followed him with her eyes. Was it apparent she liked this guy or what?

In the spirit of Matchmaking 101, I called on her and this young man during one of my talks. He came bounding up. She turned five shades of red and moved slowly up to the podium. We spoke of the girl-meets-guy thing, and I had them be my objects of illustration. They illustrated saying "Hi," holding hands, and putting-arm-around-girl scenarios. My young man volunteer was fine. The young woman? I was worried. Honestly, I thought I'd made a big mistake. What if she fainted on us, right up here in front of everyone? How would I explain it to her parents? Well, we finished our little visual aid part of the lesson, and they were excused to take their seats in the chapel. At the conclusion of the conference, a couple of my little volunteer's friends came up to me. They thanked me for calling on their friend. "She *likes* him!" they said. I told a little white lie. "Oh, really? I hadn't noticed." "Yes! And because of you, he asked her to dance!" I had noticed that too.

"She *likes* him!" they said. And it was obvious. Now, if they had started dating and he had all kinds of good qualities that impressed her, she would still be liking him. And if he continued to give her heart palpitations and she would give him the world, she would *still* be liking him. It would be dangerous for her to think there was more to it than that. Same goes for him. Love is like plus something. Like plus honesty. Like plus sacrifice. Like plus spiritual sharing. Like plus a desire to be your very best. A few ways you may know you are experiencing love are:

> You are ready to make sacrifices with an unselfish heart.

You are secure and confident about the future.
You are ready to face realistic problems.
There is growth of common interests and deepening of feelings.
You are able to share deeply spiritual feelings and goals.
You are able to be honest without fear of rejection.
You want the very best for him or her.
You want to be your very best because of his or her influence.
You think this person will make a wonderful and worthy parent.
You are proud of him or her and what he or she represents.
You share high ideals and celestial goals.
You want to be worthy of going to the temple with this person.

If you are having inappropriate feelings, take a step back and reevaluate so that you don't move too fast. Randy Bird, a wonderful teacher and curriculum developer for the Church Educational System, once shared a funny poem about moving too quickly. This is how it goes:

Indian Love Poem

Nice night, In June
Star shine, Big moon
In park, On bench
With girl, In clench.
Me say, "Me love"
She coo, Like dove.
Me smart. Me fast.
Never let, Chance pass.
"Get hitched" Me say.
She say "Okay."
Wedding bells Ring. Ring.
Honeymoon. Everything.
Settle down, Married life.
Everything, Happy life.

> 'Nother night In June,
> Stars shine, Big moon.
> No happy, No more.
> Carry baby, Walk floor.
> Wife mad, She fuss.
> Me mad. Me cuss.
> Life one, Big spat.
> Naggy wife, Bawling brat.
> Realize At last
> Me too
> Darn fast.

Randy didn't know who wrote that little gem, but it is quite a story, isn't it? Very funny but packed with potent lessons about meeting, planning, courting, and making decisions that impact us forever. The media portrayal of the moonlight-and-roses type relationship is just fine, as long as we create our love in the sunlight of Christ's standards.

The like-to-love process will happen in time. But please take your time. Meanwhile just be nice, and weigh your feelings against eternal principles. It's the only way for a natural high and the way for you to plan on a happily-ever-after.

A Few Things You Can Do

- Use the scriptures as a guide to relationships, not the television.
- Get over it. If your heart is hurting, decide it's time to get on with your life. (I know you might think, *It's easy for you to say*, but I've been there. You can do it!)
- Pray for assistance in making and keeping good friendships.
- Don't say or do things you will regret later.
- Make your firm decision on chastity now.
- Decide to be buddies with members of the opposite sex.

- Sit home rather than date someone who doesn't have your standards.
- Write down your goals toward a temple marriage; read them often.

12

Liking Yourself So Others Can Too

Have ye received his image in your countenances?
—*Alma 5:14*

Does this little song ring a bell?

I love you, you love me
We're a happy family
With a great big hug and a kiss from me to you
Won't you say you love me too?

There is a big, purple dinosaur who has taught that song to thousands of children, and many of us older folks have learned it too. Barney can really get on your nerves if you've watched him over and over and over again. (With children in my home, we have watched many an hour of that program on television over the years.) But wouldn't it honestly be great if we could walk up to our neighbor, or stop the group moving down the hall at school, or pull up alongside a car at the stoplight and sing out those words without fear of being arrested or referred to the nearest mental-health facility? I'm not advocating running up to your bishop or that cute girl in fifth period and sharing a great, big hug. Actually, it isn't the literal *saying* or *doing* of the lyrics that would be awesome, it is the *feeling* that our world could be pure and warm and open enough to allow honest expressions of love. And that we could all feel good enough about ourselves to share them!

Small children are so honest and pure in their feelings. What they *think* is what they *say*. "Hug me again,

Mommy!" or "Didn't I do a good job on my picture?" sound perfectly natural from a four-year-old. But by the time we're fourteen, it seems a bit peculiar to imagine yourself or a friend yelling out something like, "Isn't my hair *so* pretty, Daddy?" As we grow, we may lose the innocence that allows us to say what we are thinking because we might be perceived as vain or prideful or just plain weird. The "happy family"—all the world around us—seems less happy. We forget how good we really are. Why? Why do we get so discouraged because we aren't good at _____. (That blank is where you pencil in anything that makes you feel less than good.)

Little children have not yet learned that they are not good enough, pretty enough, or trained enough. They think they are wonderful! And they are. Their good feelings about themselves allow them to love and be loved. Oh, to keep that feeling the Barney set enjoys! Maybe we *can* if we work at these suggestions:

Discourage Discouragement

Picture a playground. You can see a seesaw, some swings, a slide. Children are talking to each other, easily sharing names as they laugh and play together. There is not even a thought of comparison, of segregation, of self-consciousness. As we get a little older, the doubts start to creep in and the adversary starts his ugly work in earnest, tearing away at our self-esteem.

"Susie is much prettier than I am!"

"Joe can kick the ball harder than I can!"

"Sarah has more friends than I have!"

Those kinds of comparisons are damaging and unfair. In fact, Susie and Joe and Sarah are probably looking at you and thinking about the things *you* do better than they do, and *everybody* ends up feeling lousy. The playground empties as the players become discouraged.

Satan, meanwhile, is lurking in the corner, loving every minute of our misery. "One of Satan's most powerful tools is discouragement," said Elder Marvin J. Ashton.

"Whisperings of 'you can't do it,' 'you're no good,' 'it's too late,' 'what's the use?' or 'things are hopeless' are tools of destruction." ("While They Are Waiting," *Ensign,* May 1988, p. 63.) Have you ever thought anything like that? I have. I have played right into the adversary's hands and felt miserable about myself. That utterly ungood feeling has caused me to withdraw from people around me. Everybody loses.

Get rid of the bad feelings! Turning to the One who loves us most replaces those feelings of *dis*couragement with feelings of *en*couragement. In Deuteronomy 1:21 we read, "Fear not, neither be discouraged." The Savior's way is one of *en*couragement, not *dis*couragement! Maybe we were more carefree as little children because we sincerely encouraged and applauded the strengths we saw in other people! Are we less gifted than others in many ways? Absolutely. Are there gabillions of people who can do some things better than we? Yes. And so what? Were we to look with an eye single to the glory of God, we would surely see that it is the combination of *all* our gifts and abilities that makes things run most smoothly.

There is so much to like in ourselves. Our job is to find those things and celebrate them. Almost magically, the traits we dislike in ourselves seem to disappear as we concentrate on the positive. And we become more likable in the process! If you are ready to cast off the shackles of self-doubt, you can start feeling better about who you are. Discouragement is of the devil. Don't make it easy for him. The better you feel about *you,* the better you can feel about everybody else. Replace those discouraging thoughts with positive ones, and watch your mood (and relationships) improve!

Comparisons Cannot Count

It is time for a short quiz:

- Question one: Have you gone the entire last week without comparing yourself to anyone else and feeling inadequate for the comparison?

- Question two: Do you find yourself thinking about how you wish you were as good as someone else at something?

That's it, end of quiz. (I told you it was short.)

It is pretty rare to find anyone who doesn't compare himself or herself to someone else. The interesting thing about this concept is that we generally take something weak in ourselves and compare it to some strength in another, ending up on the short end of the comparison stick. It tears us down. It robs us of self-confidence. The adversary is loving this scenario. Any way he can make us feel bad, lacking, ugly, frantic, or negative is a plus for him. While we are liking ourselves less, we are wasting time and effort that could be used in doing fun things with and for others. We could be working on improving ourselves and better understanding our friends or focusing on loving and caring about the other guy (very much like the Barney set).

Comparisons really *don't* count, unless we are making note of how much we have improved since the last time we did a personal check. Elder Neal A. Maxwell taught, "Our only valid spiritual competition is with our old selves, not with each other" (*Not My Will But Thine* [Salt Lake City: Bookcraft, 1988], p. 70). Life is hard enough for each of us. We don't need to work at making it even harder!

Work from the Inside Out

Do you feel good enough about yourself that a bad-hair day doesn't wreck your mood? Do you feel OK about yourself even if you aren't looking like the Queen of Sheba? (Actually, I've never seen the Queen of Sheba. I don't even know if she's pretty. But you get the point.) Can you give credit where credit is due, appreciating another's abilities or gifts, without feeling less worthy because of *their* accomplishments? Have you made an honest assessment of your talents, gifts, and strengths? It is important to do so if we intend to improve and progress.

"Happy is he that condemneth not himself" (Romans 14:22). With that thought in mind, let's do a personal acceptance rating:

- On a scale of one to ten, where do I rate myself overall as a person?
- What do I like best about myself?
- What do other people like best about me?
- Is there any guilt I need to get rid of? (Identify it.)
- How can I make myself a better person? (You have to do it; nobody else can.)
- Do I need an attitude adjustment?
- Would my mother freak if she saw how I act at school or at the football games?
- Do I say what I mean, or do I say what people want to hear? (In other words, am I real?)

Those are the kinds of things we need to keep track of, my friends. Not what brand of jeans we wear, how much money we make, or how our hair looks. In fact, if our self-image is tied up in how we look, what we wear, or what job or calling we have, that rating is going to fluctuate constantly. The Lord taught Samuel the importance of concerning ourselves with inner rather than outer qualities when he said, "Look not on his countenance, or on the height of his stature; . . . for the Lord seeth not as man seeth; for man looketh on the outward appearance, but the Lord looketh on the heart" (1 Samuel 16:7).

It is necessary to look on the heart to take a personal acceptance inventory. That can be a key to unlocking a more accurate, positive picture of ourselves. It has nothing to do with looking like the buff NFL quarterback or having the face or figure of a cover girl. Elder Maxwell taught it well: "We are sometimes so anxious about our personal images, when it is His image we should have in our countenances" ("'Answer Me,'" *Ensign,* November 1988, p. 31). "His image" is reflected as we work from the inside out.

Smile!

Here is a tip that pays big dividends: Smile. A lot. At many people. Not a smirky or half-hearted one. A sincere I-like-me-and-I-like-you-too one. If you're scowling, the chances aren't great that you'll attract lots of people. Nix the frown. Invite the Spirit by smiling on the inside so it can show on the outside. Or, if you're *really* in a lousy mood, maybe smiling on the *outside* will eventually lighten you up. If you want to have a good day, *make* it that way. Become more approachable by looking the part. Someone once wrote, "A smile is a light in the window of a face which shows that the heart is at home." I wish we had record of the author of those words; what a beautiful thought! In a world where some choose to be heartless, you can advertise just the opposite. You are guaranteed to receive some beautiful smiles in return. Your day will be warmer and happier. You can't help but like yourself more!

Make Note of Things You Do Well

Write down some things that you do very well. You may not include fine arts or physical talents. Using your personal acceptance rating as a foundation, flip to the end of this chapter (where you will find a blank sheet) and begin your personal competence list. Are you a good listener? List it. Do you have patience? Good, write it down. Are you a calming influence? It goes on the list. Do you keep your word? So on and so on. Whenever you think of something you do well, add it to your personal competence list. Your gratitude will increase for the good qualities you recognize, and you'll like yourself a lot more. And that increased confidence will allow better relationships, especially with the Savior.

Free Yourself from Unnecessary Guilt

Please do not feel guilty for something that is not your fault. If you have been the victim of abuse of some kind, your Heavenly Father does not hold you accountable! You must not allow yourself to think you are bad or ugly because of another's crime. Oh, please go to your bishop or another trusted leader and relieve yourself of that unnecessary burden, if needed. Promise you will. You need not spend another week or day imagining yourself to be less than you are. If there is a problem of that nature you have wrestled with, it is time to free yourself, my dear brother or sister. Choose someone who is trustworthy, and share your feelings. Allow yourself the gift of unloading the burdens in your precious, worthy heart. Get the help you need and deserve.

Get down on your knees and allow yourself to be lifted up by One who loves you so. Let him help you erase the hurts and move forward with increased confidence. I bear you testimony that the Lord hurts with you. He waits to one day hold you in his loving arms. Until such a day, he will offer you guidance and security through the gift of the Holy Ghost. Turn to him.

Forgive yourself for past transgressions. The Lord has promised us he will forgive when we repent. He has said he will forgive whom he will forgive but of us "it is required to forgive all men" (D&C 64:10). That includes ourselves. Guilt is a gift to warn us of something that needs attending to. A physical ailment causes physical pain. We realize that medical attention is needed in order to heal. A spiritual ailment causes spiritual pain. We call that pain guilt. It is a reminder that we need to heal the spiritual wound. When we deal with the transgression and correct it, we are free to spend our energies in constructive ways. Please read Alma 22:18 and commit to breaking the chains that may be breaking your heart. Once the problem is properly dealt with, it is history. It is no longer necessary (or wise) to carry the guilt. Remember, that would be Satan's way of holding us back. Move on!

Celebrate Our Divine Nature

Is there any doubt that Heavenly Father made someone great when he created you? Once you make the connection of your divine worth, you will truly begin to love yourself. It is necessary in order to really love others. Let's do a little exercise similar to a concept I have seen John Bytheway share. John is a wonderful teacher. I have heard him speak of making family connections by creating pedigree charts (you know, those sheets that old people work on to do their genealogy work). Here's a shocker: genealogy work is important for all of us; it allows us to learn more about who we are and where we come from! Let's do an experiment based on John's identity lesson: Draw a circle that represents you at the bottom of the space below. Now draw circles to represent your parents just above you. Next, draw circles representing those who are above them on the family tree. The branches could spread beyond the pages of this book and far into the distance. All those people are responsible for your genetic makeup. You are, in part, who you are because they are who *they* are. This is a picture of your mortal connection:

Now in the space below, draw a circle to represent yourself. On your spiritual family tree, who goes just above you? The circles you draw represent Heavenly Father and Heavenly Mother. There is *no one* between you and your heavenly parents! Spiritually, you are directly linked to them. You are who you are in part because they are who they are. There is a spark of divinity in you, my precious friend, for you are a child of God!

Does the term *divine nature* take on a whole new meaning for you now? Our human nature is to procrastinate, to put down, to feel bad about ourselves. Our *divine nature* allows us to rise above that and realize how good we really are. That understanding is sure to allow you to better love yourself. (Thanks, John, for making that teaching so simple to understand!)

Grow in Gratitude

Gratitude is indispensable to liking yourself more. Hartman Rector Jr. once said, "I have never seen a happy person who was not thankful" ("Success—A Journey or a Destination," *Ensign,* July 1973, p. 57). If we can "in every thing give thanks" (1 Thessalonians 5:18), we will have found a key to creating more to give thanks *for* and more to like in ourselves and in our little part of the world. Elder James E. Faust of the Quorum of the Twelve Apostles told us that "a grateful heart is a beginning of greatness" ("Gratitude As a Saving Principle," *Ensign,* May 1990, p. 86). If someone has done something nice for you today—parent, sibling, neighbor, teacher, or buddy—tell them thanks! Then turn it around and pass it on. You will feel the gratitude for being able to do something for someone else! We are capable of having wonderful, celestial relationships. It can begin by developing a more grateful heart!

Just Do It!

The bottom line for this chapter is that we must individually do the work to feel good about ourselves. We have to figure things out and do better, be better, as we go along. As our self-love grows, so does our affection and appreciation for all the other people God has made. What will you do to begin the process of better loving yourself? As you find more good in yourself, there will be more good to share with others. And your life will become much happier.

A young woman of only nineteen wrote these wise words as she was beginning her study of self-worth:

> After a while you learn the subtle difference
>   between holding a hand and chaining a soul.
> And you learn that love doesn't mean leaning and
>   company doesn't mean security.
> And you begin to learn that kisses aren't
>   contracts and presents aren't promises.
> And you begin to accept your defeats with your
>   head up and your eyes open, with the grace
>   of an adult, not the grief of a child.
> And you learn to build all your roads on today
>   because tomorrow's ground is too uncertain
>   for plans.
> After a while you learn that even sunshine burns
>   if you get too much.

> So plant your own garden and decorate your own soul, instead of waiting for someone to bring you flowers.
> And you learn that you really can endure. . . .
> That you really are strong,
> And you really do have worth.
> (Veronica A. Shoffstall, in *Chicken Soup for the Teenage Soul,* comp. Jack Canfield et al. [Deerfield Beach, Florida: Health Communications, Inc., 1997], p. 7.)

Learning to love ourselves is not necessarily easy. It is essential to finding joy, however. And it is essential for enjoying real, loving relationships with those around us. If you don't like yourself, you're missing a great relationship! Try reframing your opinion of yourself. Improve yourself daily by acting as good as you really are. Watch as your relationships grow by leaps and bounds. The more *you* like you, the more everyone else will like you!

And before we finish up here, keep in mind one more word: *acceptance.* Acceptance of our knees that are too skinny, our hair that is thinner than we wish, or our inability to get math. Acceptance of the fact that we do some things well and some things not so well. Acceptance of the package we are. There are some things we can improve upon. There are some we cannot. Change or accept. Accept weaknesses as a way to remain humble and teachable. We are given this tender encouragement in Ether 12:27: "And if men come unto me I will show unto them their weakness. I give unto men weakness that they may be humble; and my grace is sufficient for all men that humble themselves before me; for if they humble themselves before me, and have faith in me, then will I make weak things become strong unto them." None of us is bordering on being translated any time soon. How about if we relax and enjoy each other? And accept and love ourselves? Then other people can too!

A Few Things You Can Do

- Nix your negative cycle; determine that today you will be only *positive.*
- Sometime when you're in a good mood, write a nice note to yourself and stash it for a time when you need a boost.
- Write a love note to someone now and every day (it will help lift *your* mood as well as theirs).
- Pray for help in finding good things about yourself.
- Do a little something *for* yourself.
- Decide never again to compare yourself to someone else.
- Don't beat yourself up when you *do* compare. (This one may take more than a few tries!)
- Find ten scriptures that relate to your positive self-image.

Personal Competency List

13

Did You Think to Pray?

Draw near unto me and I will draw near unto you.
—D&C 88:63

To better understand prayer," explained Elder Richard G. Scott of the Quorum of the Twelve Apostles, "I have listened to the counsel of others, pondered the scriptures, and studied the lives of prophets and others. Yet what seems most helpful is seeing in my mind a child approaching trustingly a loving, kind, wise, understanding Father, who wants us to succeed. Don't worry about your clumsily expressed feelings. Just talk to your Father. He hears every prayer and answers it in His way." ("Learning to Recognize Answers to Prayer," *Ensign*, November 1989, pp. 30–31.)

You might have noticed that at the end of each chapter under the header "A Few Things You Can Do" prayer is listed as a go-and-do thing. No matter what else you think, say, or do to improve your relationships and your life in general, *prayer* will get you closer to your goals and help you appreciate them more. We didn't get into studying prayer in our communication chapter because we need more than a paragraph or two! I hope you're ready for a sit-and-think part of our book experience. To better understand and appreciate this means of communication between us and our Father takes some real pondering.

We aren't talking the Prayer 101 routine. You know, "Heavenly Father, I thank thee for . . . Please bless . . . In the name of Jesus Christ, amen." The same words in the same places day in and day out. The yes-I-said-my-prayers prayer, as though it can be crossed off our list now and we won't have a guilty conscience. We are talking *real prayer*. Communication between us and Father. Opening the heart and letting it all out. Asking questions and waiting to feel the Spirit's promptings. Conversing just like a little child would with his or her loving Father. I like what Alonzo A. Hinckley said: "My father prayed; he didn't say his prayers" (in Conference Report, April 1934, p. 53). What a difference between the two!

The Savior counsels us to "watch ye therefore, and pray always" so that we can be "accounted worthy" (Luke 21:36). All the subjects we have talked about in this little workbook *need* prayerful consideration in order to work in our lives. As a recap, let's take a few minutes to concentrate on how prayer can help in these areas of bettering our relationships.

Liking Yourself

True esteem comes from knowing Father better and reflecting on his love for us. Too often I have heard someone say, "I can't pray; I'm not worthy" or "God won't hear my prayers." What a bunch of baloney! He loves perfectly, my friend. He may loathe an action that has been taken, but he loves the one who chose to act that way. His ears are always tuned to hear us. And he will answer, as long as we remember that prayer is a two-way street of communication. Making the effort to talk with him is a major step in the right direction.

Imagine that you and Brenda are best friends. Brenda's dad gets a new job, so they have to move far away. You are initially crushed to be apart from your friend, but you promise that you will talk by phone every day, morning and night. After the move your phone conversations go like this:

"Brenda, hi, this is Kim! Just called to say good morning and I love you!" Then you hang up. Brenda is left standing with the receiver in her hand thinking, *Well, that was a great conversation!* (Not.) That night you ring up Brenda again:

"Brenda, it's me, Kim. Just wanted to let you know I'm thinking of you and hope you had a good day. I did! Bye!" You hang up the phone.

Next day you call again. "Brenda, this is Kim. I had a good night's sleep last night. Now I have to take off for school or I'm gonna be late." Click.

That night it is a repeat performance: "Brenda, it's Kim. I'm really grateful for our friendship and I love you. Gotta go!" The phone goes dead.

How is Brenda feeling after two or three weeks of this? Don't you think she is wondering if they even *have* any relationship? What kind of friend calls you, says a few repetitive words, doesn't give you a chance to get a word in edgewise, and then hangs up the receiver? Both friends have missed out on meaningful communication. And Kim has never heard what Brenda had to say, probably missing out on some important information.

If you have your spiritual eyes and ears tuned, you understand how similar our prayers can be to the Brenda–Kim relationship. If you get down on your knees and check in every morning and evening, that's good. But if you are saying essentially the same things without giving thought to your prayer as an actual conversation, how are you able to open your heart and come closer to Heavenly Father? If you hang up the receiver by bouncing up off your knees as soon as you have said amen, how can Father tell you anything? Prayer is *two-way communication.* If we are jumping up and running off without giving time for answers to come, we are losing out on some important information. Leaving that line open for loving answers will allow us to improve in feelings of self-worth and like ourselves so much more!

Standards

The scriptures say, "Pray always, that you may come off conqueror" (D&C 10:5). Let's talk briefly of fairy tales here. Fairy tales always have a hero. They also have a villain, a mean and ugly, miserable, good-for-nothing lowlife. The hero battles the villain. The hero always wins, but not right off the bat. First the hero meets obstacles and has to regroup. He or she must rely on having the source of truth on his or her side so that injustice can be obliterated. Finally, after a lengthy battle and with truth and righteousness at his or her side, the hero wins! They all live happily ever after. The end.

In this mortal life, *you* are the hero or heroine. The villain you must battle is known as Satan. He is good for nothing and is out to make you miserable in the end. He can do that by dulling your senses and lowering your standards. The obstacles that keep you from living happily ever after are placed there by him. If you go into battle by yourself, you will *lose*. I cannot emphasize that enough. You will *lose* your battle if you go against the villain unarmed regarding movies, books, activities, dress standards, Word of Wisdom, or anything.

Going into battle with truth and righteousness will arm you for coming off conqueror. Your sources of truth and help are Father in Heaven and the Savior. They are there to help *win* the battle. *Prayer* is the way we receive the strength and armor of righteousness needed to *win every time*. Satan doesn't stand a chance of messing with our standards if we are prayerful and careful. And remember, "Father knoweth what things ye have need of, before ye ask" (Matthew 6:8). Ask, and he is waiting to bless!

Feelings

We sing, "Prayer is the soul's sincere desire" (*Hymns*, no. 145). Our heart's desires are known by Father anyway; why don't we go to him in prayer so that he can help us? Because he knows exactly how we are feeling, he is more able to help us than anyone else. At those times when you are confused or torn apart or heartbroken, your faith will be strengthened and understanding increased.

I have known of no one whose faith in her friend was any stronger than a friend I'll call Sandy. Sandy served a faithful mission and then returned home to move forward with her life. She found a wonderful young man, and they fell in love and made plans to marry. Because I knew that Sandy wanted more than anything to be an honorable wife and mother, I was thrilled for her. The marriage took place, and some months later I heard that Sandy was going to be a mother. Again, I was so happy for her! Soon the time had come for Sandy's baby to be born.

At the time when a little one makes his or her entrance into mortality, there is a great energy and excitement in the delivery room. On this morning in Sandy's delivery room, that energy was strangely subdued. When the doctor placed Sandy's newborn in her arms, it was clear that this baby would not be like most. This little one would have physical and mental limitations that would take their toll on the baby and the parents. The nurses were so sad for this new mother and father. As Sandy held her new little baby, tears came down her cheeks and she whispered, "Heavenly Father sent me a perfect one! He sent me a perfect one!"

Sandy's faithful relationship with our Truest Friend helped her understand that all would be well. What a lesson she taught in the delivery room that day! Now, several years later, Sandy is indeed a good and loving mom and cherishes each day with her precious child. From the day that baby was born, Sandy's *feelings* were in line with what the Savior would want. It has helped her so much in her daily life!

Can you see how, if we have established powerful channels of inspiration through prayer, we can get through whatever challenges lie before us? We are able to find the silver linings in those storm clouds that sometimes close in on us. Our feelings about ourselves and the people we know become more charitable. Our take on the whole life experience becomes more valuable because our feelings are more in harmony with Christ's.

Communication

Communication is where prayer really makes a difference in dramatic ways because people will respond better to you as you prayerfully consider how to better respond to them! Prayer will help you to change. Prayer will help you to understand that *other* people may change if you do. Prayer might be the only thing that gets you through some tough spots when you don't think you are capable of communicating civilly or effectively.

"Prayer is the instrument of miracles," President Marion G. Romney of the First Presidency once said (quoted in Devere Harris, "Spiritual Power," *Ensign,* November 1984, p. 27). We can really see miracles happen in our relationships as we prayerfully consider how to make things better.

K.I.S.S. Principles

To be *kind,* to get more *involved,* to have that great *sense of humor,* to live a life of *service* requires that our prayer quotient increase.

- How are you going to be able to be kind to someone you can barely tolerate if you don't petition heaven through prayer?
- If you are shy or are suffering from the I-can't-do-this syndrome (which, by the way, the adversary loves), how will you take that deep breath and make a giant step forward without the Lord's help?
- Maybe you never thought that Heavenly Father would answer your prayers to increase your sense of humor, but he will. After all, he wants you to be happy (2 Nephi 2:25 tells us, "Men are, that they might have joy"). A sense of humor is not a frivolous thing to ask of him, and surely he has a perfect sense of humor!
- Growth in your service quotient will most likely be proportionate to your prayerful seeking for opportunities to work at making someone's day better.

I like what President Thomas S. Monson of the First Presidency once said about prayer and work: "A mammoth 747 jetliner, while flying over the Pacific, sustained a gigantic tear in its side, ejecting nine passengers to their deaths and threatening the lives of all. When the pilot, Captain David Cronin, was interviewed, having brought the craft back safely to Honolulu, he was asked, 'What did you do when the plane ripped open? How did you cope?' Captain Cronin replied, 'I prayed, then went to work.' My brethren, this is an inspired plan for each of us to follow: Pray, and then go to work." ("Go For It!" *Ensign*, May 1989, p. 44.)

So let's get to work prayerfully on those four principles!

Friendships

The best friends I've ever had are the ones who share my same feelings of reverence for sacred things. Regardless of religious affiliation, they believe in Christ, worship God, and base their lives on prayerful decision making. Because they are more focused on important things, I have felt comfortable that our friendship was more substantial.

Shirley and I met when I was twelve years old and newly moved to Hampton, Virginia. We have maintained a loving friendship that grows more and more in value through the years. Although Shirley attends a different church, we share the same spiritual foundation. I could feel comfortable kneeling in prayer with her. In fact, I have no doubt that there have been times when she has petitioned the Lord in my behalf. I love the feeling that she cares enough to do the things that matter most! Think about your circle of friends. The relationships that will last are the ones fixed upon spiritual roots. You deserve the kind of friends who will pray with and for you. Birds of a feather really *do* flock together!

Romance

Have you heard the stories that begin, "When I was a young girl, we *never* . . ." or "When I was young, we guys *always* . . ." Back in the olden days things seemed a lot more simple. But I bet that if the truth were known finding and keeping true love was just as hard back then as it is now. The circumstances have shifted and the world's immoral influences have gotten stronger, but a substantial love still needs the same tender attention as it did a hundred years ago.

Elder James E. Talmage once said, "The prayer of the heart is greater than the prayer of the lips" (in Conference Report, October 1931, p. 50). Likewise, the relationship of the heart is greater than a relationship of the lips! To insure a real love when that times comes, it has to be based upon prayerful consideration of eternal principles. No matter how much you enjoy holding hands or kissing lips, you must go to the heart of the matter for a love that lasts.

I found a Latin proverb that goes like this, "Govern your passions, or they will govern you." Prayerfully seeking the Lord's direction will allow us to *govern* ourselves. That means we can *manage, control,* and properly *influence* ourselves. By taking care of the physical element that might want to leap out way early in a relationship, we are free to love *better.* Elder Hartman Rector Jr. of the Seventy said it this way: "Those who are the best love the best" (in Conference Report, October 1969, p. 76). Creating and keeping a strong relationship can be hard work. Making it a celestial one takes even more work. Prayer is the cornerstone of building a love in which we can "be comforted, being knit together in love" (Colossians 2:2).

OK, you guys. We just had a recap of some of the important areas that need working on or reworking to help these relationships of ours become more celestial. In order to move in a more heavenly direction, we have got to get closer to heaven, and that comes by way of prayer.

If I could take the feelings out of my heart and put them directly into yours, I would want you to know that there is more comfort and reassurance and direction to be found in prayer than by any other means. It is truly the key to unlocking many of our questions and getting rid of our frustrations, or at least helping us deal with those frustrations. I agree with the words of Alfred Lord Tennyson: "More things are wrought by prayer than this world dreams of."

Take these few words and place them securely in your heart: "Ere you left your room this morning, did you think to pray?" (*Hymns,* no. 140.) The words to that hymn stuck in my heart a lot of years ago. When I awake in the mornings, there is this instant replay that goes off. I see the words run across the screen in my mind from time to time throughout the day. It is my personal reminder that I need to pray in order to make it as good a day as possible. At best, it is the foundation for little miracles to occur. At the least, it is a humbling blessing to put things in better perspective. Maybe you can place those same lyrics in the instant replay of your brain. And keep in mind the kind, loving Father who wants to hear from you and delights in answering your prayers!

14

It's Worth the Effort!

*Remember that it is upon the rock of our Redeemer . . .
that ye must build your foundation.*
—Helaman 5:12

Whew! We have covered a lot of territory, my friend. This is just about where I leave you, and it is at this point that you pick from among the things I have shared, apply any just-for-you inspirations that have come to you, make use of added insights from specific scriptures, and make your relationship so much better. It is time to *do* something with the added knowledge. Remember, *knowing* is not enough! Compare these three takes on doing:

> Don't just stand there—do something
> (Anonymous).
> Don't just do something—stand there
> (George Shulz).
> Don't just stand there—undo something
> (Murray Weidenbaum).

No doubt we know people who fit each category and have probably found that we fit quite well in each from time to time. But this time, let's choose category one. We were meant to succeed. The Lord wants us to. He has provided all the tools to make sure that we do. Are you ready to succeed?

What Is Success?

What is success?
To laugh often and much;

> To win the respect of intelligent people
> and the affection of little children;
> To earn the appreciation of honest critics
> and endure the betrayal of false friends;
> To appreciate beauty,
> To find the best in others
> To leave the world a bit better, whether by
> a healthy child, a garden patch,
> or a redeemed social condition;
> To know even one life has breathed
> easier because you have lived;
> This is to have succeeded.
> —Ralph Waldo Emerson

Isn't that a great poem? With those thoughts coupled with the Savior's teachings that are at our disposal, we cannot do anything but succeed! We can be thrilled for our successes and just as happy about the accomplishments of our friends. Can you imagine how great it would be to live in a world where no one gets caught up in the nanny-nanny-boo-boo syndrome of the I-win-therefore-you-lose cycle?

There are no losers. That is a deceit and a lie perpetrated by the devil. Our world of competition and awards and who's who is not in keeping with our Heavenly Father's plan. His kingdom is large enough to hold all of us. His love provides for equal security and blessings for every single one. Your heavenly parents would create children born to win, wouldn't they? That means *you*. *You* were born to win, to win "all things that the Father hath" (John 16:15).

Your friends and family were born to that same heritage. It is a birthright for each and every one. Do you not *deserve* to treat yourself with respect and love? Shouldn't it be expected that we treat others that way too?

Next time you're in a room full of people at school, at work, or at a ball game, look around. Every girl in that room is some man's queen. Each man in that area is some woman's king. Each of us, born of heavenly parents, are bound for celestial blessings if we remember who we are and what we are about. *That* should make us think and speak and act accordingly. Christ has been the example for us to follow. The promised blessings are well worth the effort to follow his guidelines. They will not eliminate all our problems or heartaches, but they will help us process them properly.

He is always watching over us, always closer than we might expect and waiting for us to learn that for ourselves. My teenage son David learned that lesson when, in April of 1996, he was crossing the main road that runs in front of our church building. He and a group of friends had been practicing for a ward lip-sync contest, and David was returning home. I'll spare you the gory details, but David was hit by a car. His body was hit by a Lexus traveling at a decent rate of speed. The accident tossed him into the air, flipped him over a couple of times, and dumped him on the pavement of 2300 East in Salt Lake City. It was one of those this-can't-be-happening experiences.

The emergency vehicles came from every direction, and the EMT called ahead to the hospital to say they had a severe head-trauma patient coming in. They didn't know if he was going to make it or not. He was taken on a stretcher with those blow-up pads all around him to stabilize his body. He was bloody and bruised. There is much I could share with you concerning that accident, my friends, but this is what I need you to know: When I rushed into the hospital emergency room to see David, I was shocked. He was alert and calm. In the very center of my being, I knew he was going to be OK.

The bottom line was that although his sternum was cracked, he had a goose egg over his right eye, his knees and legs were banged up, and the skin was gone from his entire arm, he was OK. Not a bone was broken. When he made the flip that landed him on the ground, he should have hit on the right side of the top of his head. At that place his hair was mowed down to about an inch and a half high. It literally looked like a tiny lawn mower had scraped over that area. There was not a scratch on his scalp. There was not a cut or a bruise above his brain.

That day I looked at my son and said, "David, you must never forget this day. Heavenly Father obviously desires you to live, for you should have been gone. This mark on your hair is as though the angels themselves carried you so that your head did not take the brunt of the force of your fall. Never forget how you were watched over and protected today."

David learned for himself that day that the Lord's tender watchcare was over him. It has made a difference in the way he looks at things and in the way he relates to others. It has served him well in learning how important he is to his Father in Heaven.

Likewise, Heavenly Father has his watchcare over *you* and me. The very angels often are surrounding us, assisting us in our efforts to do good. Although the outcome may not always be what we would choose, it is always the best thing for us. You and I don't have to get through this life or deal with these relationship things on our own. The Savior and all those who love and work with him are ready to assist, desirous of our success. All of these learning and growing experiences are not solo ventures; we can feel secure in our Father's watchcare.

For several years I served on the board of directors for Utah Special Olympics. My friend Steve James and I cowrote the theme song for the Special Olympics program on a state-by-state basis. That honor allowed me to mingle with and learn from those special people who are participants in the program. What great things they can teach us!

My dear friend Bart, who is a Special Olympian, has taught me the joy of being enthusiastic. Bart was born with mental and physical handicaps. His communication abilities are like those of a small child. His body is twisted and bent so that his height is 5'8" or 5'9" instead of the 6'2" he should probably be. He has endured many challenges, but he always smiles. Several years ago I was able to be in attendance when Bart received his Eagle Scout award. At the time he was about thirty years old. The grown men who had worked with him and learned from him wept because of their love for Bart. At the reception following the ceremony, Bart came down the steps of the stage into the cultural hall and made a beeline for Steve and me. He put his hands on Steve's shoulders and said in his halting, hard-to-understand voice, "Remember who you are. Heavenly Father loves you!" I will never forget the feeling that enveloped me from head to toe. His words were hard to understand, but the Spirit's influence was perfectly clear. Bart was steady and firm in the things that matter most. His beautiful spirit radiated love and joy. His enthusiasm for life and for the gospel was awesome.

How is your enthusiasm level? The more you can inch it upward, the more success you will enjoy. To be like Bart is a goal of mine. He has learned that "the eyes of the Lord are over the righteous, and his ears are open unto their prayers" (1 Peter 3:12).

I was thinking back on my life in high school. That was about a hundred years ago or so; you know, when we had to walk five miles to and from school uphill both ways? My mind wandered to the time I started cheerleading and how it taught me a love of sports. From eighth grade through my senior year of high school, I did the cheerleading thing. So I had plenty of time to watch football and basketball. By the time I got to twelfth grade, I knew all about the rules of those sports. I became totally involved in the games and screamed and jumped and hopped around as though my energy would make all the difference in the game's outcome. I realize how goofy I must have acted, but I sure had a good time. Now I realize that I started loving sports because through cheerleading I got closer, took a personal interest, and got caught up in the games. All these years later, you might hear me three blocks away at certain championship games. I'm not as limber as I used to be, and I wouldn't dream of attempting a C jump or anything, but my lungs are just as loud and energetic as ever! It's scary and more than a little embarrassing for the rest of my family. I, however, get a big kick out of throwing myself into the moment.

If I throw my energy into the things that I grow closer to, to the things and people I take a more personal interest in, I can get caught up in the things that will make for a better life with better relationships. (Remember, relationships are the most important thing!) Let's get caught up in life; not in the world, but in living life so that we can enjoy life eternal.

Well, we're just about finished up here. If there is one more thing I would like to say before saying "Goodbye for now," it is this: *keep at it!* When things get really hard and you feel like giving up or throwing in the towel, keep at it. Relationships worth having for eternity are worth working at. Don't give up. Don't chicken out. Don't put yourself on hold for months because something lousy happened. "Press forward with a steadfastness in Christ, having a perfect brightness of hope" (2 Nephi 31:20).

The first time I drove the family car without adult supervision was one of those I-think-I'll-bag-this-whole-thing experiences. I took a couple of my friends up to the 7-Eleven. You can't imagine how nervous I was. Well, maybe you can. Trying to be cool, I took a deep breath and acted like I knew exactly what I was doing. All went well until I pulled into the parking lot of the convenience store. Then I got the foot pedals confused in my mind. I slammed on the gas instead of putting on the brakes! We came within three or four inches of plowing through the pane-glass front of the 7-Eleven. I was too embarrassed (and shook up) to even get out of the car, and when the others came back outside I asked one of them to drive back home. At that point I was definitely *not* feeling cool. It freaked me out so much that I wouldn't drive again for almost a full year!

How much like life was that experience! Going full-steam ahead, we think we have everything under control. In an instant, we come so close to disaster. Sometimes it is our wake-up call. It spurs us to move forward and do what needs to be done. Other times, it may scare us so much that we are afraid to move forward with our lives. At those times it would be good to remember 2 Nephi 31:20.

At this point, I am hoping there are lots of marks in this book and lots of goals you have made. It is worth the effort for the joy you will experience. I have, no doubt, written imperfectly. But the principles I have written about *are* perfect. And they are guaranteed to improve the way you relate.

I want you to be happy. To be kind and involved in life. To have a healthy sense of humor and a service mentality. I hope you will get in touch with your feelings and allow others to have theirs. I desire you to understand that pretty is as pretty does, that better communication can do wonders for your relationships, that your standards will make or break you. I pray you will like yourself so that other people can like you even more and that you will properly prepare for an eternal romance based on the principles that will bring you absolute joy. I hope you choose friends wisely and draw ever closer to your truest friend.

I'm off to go and do now. Won't you do the same? If we have an opportunity to meet, will you let me know how you're doing on this relationship thing? I am rooting for you. Much more importantly, the Savior is rooting for you. He is our example. His teachings are our guidelines for better relationships. "Remember that it is upon the rock of our Redeemer, who is Christ, the Son of God, that ye must build your foundation; that when the devil shall send forth his mighty winds, yea, his shafts in the whirlwind, yea, when all his hail and his mighty storm shall beat upon you, it shall have no power over you to drag you down to the gulf of misery and endless wo, because of the rock upon which ye are built, which is a sure foundation, a foundation whereon if men build they cannot fall" (Helaman 5:12).

We *cannot fall!* As the Lord is my witness, I promise you that you will see miracles happen in your life as you follow his guidelines. Keep that Hershey Kiss thought in your mind and the Lord's teachings in your heart.

Thanks for taking the time and effort to read these words. I sure hope they have been of some help to you! I bear you my testimony that the Lord lives and loves us.

My brother, will you do whatever it takes to be worthy of a queen? My sister, will you put forth the effort to be fit for a king? If we will each do our part, our relationships will become more heavenly. And we may look forward to the day when we will share in the joy of that celestial kingdom that awaits at the end of this mortal journey. Isn't that where kings and queens should reside?

Remember, we are meant to succeed. With a lot of hard work and a lot of real prayer, we will. In the end, we will learn for ourselves that it is worth the effort!

Index

— A —

Abed-nego, story of, 75–76
Abraham, 70
Acceptance, 114
Adversity, 76
Afflictions, 76
Andrea, story of move to Utah, 9
Anger, 55
Antique dealer, story of, 20
Antrim, Minna, on experience, 4
Aristotle, on bravery, 80
Ashton, Marvin J., on commitment, 24
  on discouragement, 105–6
  on how the Lord measures us, 40
  on love, 63
Attitudes, 6, 66
  positive, 88
  worldly, 35

— B —

Baby's birth, story of, 120–21
Backman, Robert L., on relationships, 98–99
Bacon, Francis, on revenge, 60
Ballard, M. Russell, on attitude, 6
Bart, story of earning Eagle, 129–30
Beauty, 64
Benson, Ezra Taft, on joyful living, 66–67
  on kindness, 10

Boy hit by car, story of, 128–29
Brad, story of conversion, 70–71
Brain tumor, story of woman with, 93
Bravery, 80
Brown, Hugh B., 30
Browning, Robert, on heaven, 39

— C —

Celestial feelings, 52
Celestial relationships, 113, 124
Charity, 11
Chastity, 99
Cheerfulness, 67
Choosing, 3
Christiansen, ElRay L., on judging, 66
Commandments, 69
Commitment, 24
Communication, 49, 54–60, 119, 121–22
Communication skills, 57–58
Comparing self, 106–7
Cosmetics, 64
Cousins, Norman, on laughter, 32
Cruelty, 10

— D —

Dances, 18–19
Dating, 79–82
  steady, 98
David, story of accident, 128–29

135

David the king, 99
Dead Poets Society (movie), story of watching, 89
Decisions, 81
Differences, celebrating, 45
Discouragement, 106
Dishonesty, 56
Divine nature, 111
Dress standards, 77–78

— E —

Eagle Scout, story of handicapped man earning, 129–30
Embarrassment, stories of, 84–85
Emerson, Ralph Waldo, on friends, 88
  poem, 126–27
Emotional feelings, 49
Emotions, 45, 55
  sharing of, 89
Entertainment, 76–77
Eternal relationships, 95
Exercise, 4

— F —

Faust, James E., on gratitude, 113
Feelings, 132
  celestial, 52
  emotional, 49
  expression of, 60
  physical, 48
  sharing of, 89
Forgiveness, 59
Friends, 60, 83–95
Friendships, 123
  cultivation of, 86

— G —

Genetic makeup, 111
Girls and guys, difference between, 44–46
Girl with fatal kidney ailment, story of, 92

Good Samaritan, The, 41
Gratitude, 112–13
Guilt, 109–10

— H —

Half-heartedness, 22
Hanks, Marion D., on example, 47–48
Happiness, 108
Hearts, Lord's measurement of, 40
Heart specialist, story of unkept, 65
HELLP syndrome, story of woman with, 92–93
Hershey's kisses, 2
Hinckley, Alonzo A., on prayer, 118
Hinckley, Gordon B., on attitude, 66
  on religion of the media, 21–22
  on Ten Commandments, 74
Holy Ghost, 79
Honesty, 56–57
Hoyt, Daniel W., poem by, 60
Hugo, Victor, on laughter, 90
Humiliation, 83
Humility, 67–68
Humor, sense of, 26–34, 122

— I —

Image, 108
Immorality, 99
"Indian Love Poem", 101–2
Introductions, 96–97
Involvement, 17–25

— J —

Jesus, focus on, 92
  on kissing, 2
  trusting in, 94
Joseph, 99
Joshua, on choosing, 3
Judging others, 65–66

Index

— K —

Kapp, Ardeth G., on pulling together, 81
Keller, Helen, on feeling, 4
Kimball, J. Golden, story of his humor, 90
Kimball, Spencer W., on decision making, 75
  on humility, 68–69
  on kissing, 2
  on loving others, 57
  on morality, 74
  on service, 42
Kindheartedness, 8
Kindness, 8–16
  definition of, 9–10
  practicing, 90
King David, 99
Kissing, 2
"Kissing", poem, 1
Koppel, Ted, on Ten Commandments, 74

— L —

Laughter, 26–34, 89–90
  a blessing, 29
"Lifting and Learning" (poem), 58–59
Liking yourself, 118–19
Listening, 56
Love, 98–99, 124
  of self, 88, 104–14
  ways to know you are experiencing, 100–101
Loving others, 62–71
Lust, 98–99

— M —

Mailee, story of helping new girl, 9
Margaret, story of fainting, 36–37
Marquis, Don, on understanding women, 44
Maxwell, Neal A., on anger, 55
  on being half-hearted, 22
  on being involved, 21
  on humor, 29
  on image, 108
  on sense of humor, 30
  on spiritual competition, 107
McKay, David O., on dealing with others, 9
  on gender roles, 47
  on life, 14
Meshach, story of, 75–76
Michael, story of befriending a girl, 14–15
Milk shakes, story of fly in, 77
Monson, Thomas S., on prayer, 122–23
Moroni, 88

— O —

Orben, Robert, on exercise, 4

— P —

Pahnke, Vickey, story of being sent to principle, 30–31
  story of falling in church, 83–84
  story of wearing different shoes, 32–33
Passions, 124
Pearson, Carol Lynn, on love, 50
Perry, L. Tom, on being a righteous husband, 47
Perry, Steven K., on evening gowns, 78
Physical feelings, 48
Positive attitude, 88
Prayer, 117–25
Prototype friends, 86–87

— R —

Rector, Hartman Jr., on gratitude, 112–13
  on love, 124
Relationship problems, 3
Relationships 099 class, 3

Relationships, 3–7, 131
　celestial, 113, 124
　eternal, 95
　proper, 99
Religion of the media, 21–22
Repentance, 110
Respect, 58, 127
Responsibility, 57
Romance, 97–102, 123–24
Romney, Marion G., on prayer, 122

— S —

Sandy, story of, 120–21
Sarcasm, 10
Scott, Richard G., on prayer, 117
Self, comparing to others, 106–7
　liking, 118–19
Self-confidence, 18
Self-discipline, 69
Self-love, 113
Self-worth, 104–14, 118–19
Sense of humor, 89–90
　and prayer, 122
　story of couple's, 29–30
Service, 35–43
　benefits of, 42
Shadrach, story of, 75–76
Shoes, story of wearing different, 32–33
Shoffstall, Veronica A., on self-worth, 113–14
Silence, 55
Smiling, 109
Smith, George Albert, on kind deeds, 9
Standards, 73–82, 119–20
　dress, 77–78
"Stand or Fall" (song), lyrics, 80
Steady dating, 98
St. Francis of Assisi, on attitude, 88
Success, 126–27, 129

— T —

Talmage, James E., on prayer, 124
Tanner, N. Eldon, on honoring womanhood, 47
Temples, 75
Tennyson, Alfred Lord, on prayer, 125
"The Last Touch", poem, 50–51
"The Snob", story, 12–14
Time, for service, 39
Tina, story of bad mood, 91
Trust, 56
Truth, 57
Two-two-one theory, 56

— U —

Unkindness, 29

— V —

Volunteer work, 40

— W —

Wallflowers, 19
Wedding disasters, story of reading, 33
Wesley, John, on doing good, 39
"What Is Success?", poem, 126–27
Wig falling off, story of, 85
Wilcox, Ella Wheeler, "Lifting and Learning," 58–59
Wirthlin, Joseph B., on keeping commandments, 73–74

— Y —

Young, Brigham, on feeding others, 39
　on womanhood, 47